# A Travel Agent in Cyber School

# A Travel Agent in Cyber School: The Internet and the Library Media Program

John F. LeBaron
Catherine Collier
Linda de Lyon Friel

1997
Libraries Unlimited, Inc.
Englewood, Colorado

LIBRARIES UNLIMITED, INC.
P.O. Box 6633
Englewood, CO 80155-6633
1-800-237-6124


Constance Hardesty
*Project Editor*

Jane Olivier
*Production*

Sheryl Tongue
*Design and Layout*

**Library of Congress Cataloging-in-Publication Data**

LeBaron, John, 1939–
    A travel agent in cyber school : the Internet and the library
media program / John F. LeBaron, Catherine Collier, Linda de Lyon
Friel.
    xxi, 170 p.  17×25 cm.
    ISBN 1-56308-333-7
    1. School libraries--United States--Data processing.   2. Internet
(Computer network)   3. Library information networks--United States.
I. Collier, Catherine.   II. Friel, Linda de Lyon, 1948–   .
III. Title
Z675.S3L38515   1996
027.8′ 0285--DC20                                          96-31826
                                                              CIP

# Contents ■

# Figures ■

# Tables ■

# Foreword ■

**DURING A RECENT CONVERSATION WITH A YOUNG COLLEAGUE**, she lamented that not much had happened throughout the twenty-plus years of her life. Few new inventions had come to the forefront, such as those that had changed the lives of the previous generation—electricity, the automobile, computers, television. Apparently she did not recognize the information revolution as either exciting or life-changing. My astonishment was tempered by the realization that the rapid race into the information age has had more to do with knowing than with doing, and if you did not know that you were missing something, the change was apparently transparent. The refinements and not-so-subtle changes my colleague missed portend transformation of every aspect of life into the twenty-first century.

Nobody came close to predicting the social, economic, and cultural impact that previous inventions were to have on life on this planet. Consider the printing press, or the transistor. On a more mundane note, could we have forecast the changes wrought by the invention of the automobile? Now, parents of teenagers fret wakefully if the sound of tires wheeling into the driveway fails to materialize by midnight. The landscape is laced with long asphalt ribbons. City streets become gridlocked.

No one can predict with certainty how our lives, learning, and play will be changed by the Internet—but change they most certainly will. Electronic access to information in text, visual, and aural formats exponentially broadens horizons in one fell swoop! It reduces time and distance and eliminates many of the previous barriers these factors posed. Educationally, it enables new teaching techniques, groupings, environments, and even sites that will have a profound effect on individual learning styles and preferences.

Media librarians have long been encouraged to be active participants in the structural changes occurring in their educational institutions by assuming the role of change agent. Many have accepted the challenge to improve teaching and learning. Today they are joined by children who are growing up with media and technology exposures and experiences every day, eventually coming to school with new and different skills, preferences, and learning styles. One example is the ease with which very young children manipulate and understand the meaning of symbols and icons. Children are now living and playing in rich information environments that are as extensive as they are chaotic.

Understanding that different disciplines store their information differently, use unique vocabularies, and in general organize their knowledge bases to suit their professionals, media librarians are well prepared to be pathfinders and trailblazers. Trained to know where to look, what to look for, how best to search specific arenas, and which sources are best for which inquiries, media librarians are ready for today's challenge.

Educational institutions need only recognize that help is readily available to teach students and teachers how to build appropriate pathways to and through the exploding information universe. They also need to recognize that information is the means to knowledge and not an end in itself. Recent research linking student achievement with the presence of professionally staffed library media centers speaks not to the facility, but rather to the program and its attendant human interaction, which encourages students to explore, inquire, question, test, and expand their knowledge based on wide access to information.

School library media centers exist to further the education of youth by ensuring that students and staff are effective users of ideas and information. Until recent years, this meant relying on in-house information, or, at most, nearby public or college libraries. Assignments were made based on the knowledge that students would have to spend most of their time finding sufficient information, leaving little time for them to process and craft new knowledge.

Today we are no longer on the cusp of an age, but *in* the maelstrom of an exploding universe. The importance of the media librarian and the major information tool, the Internet, cannot be overstated. For where are we heading? Toward the creation of new knowledge, based on thoughtful assessments of a variety of viewpoints, conflicting ideas and conclusions, and numerous competing theories—assessments that are now possible because of the ready availability of full-text resources, particularly the Internet. Nor are we still limited only to print!

The "Net," however, is far more than just an electronic information source. It is a veritable communication village that connects people and places in ways previously not possible. The learner connects directly with decision makers, inventors, scientists, artists, and others. No intermediary need offer an explanation, cloud or twist an issue. However, learners must maintain their vigilance regarding issues of authenticity and ownership. The Net effectively shortens distance, compresses time, and makes Netters aware of their global capabilities. It recognizes no time or place boundaries, and often language barriers are eliminated. This alone has the potential to reshape our current learning patterns. No longer tied to a six-hour day, or the time constraints of contacting individuals halfway around the globe, learning can become an unending experience.

The rich treasures of the Internet almost beg to be explored. Students are eager to exploit the Net; teachers are concerned that students' time and intellect be productively used. *A Travel Agent in Cyber School* provides the ticket and many optional routes to explore and investigate. The fundamentals of the Internet are presented for your exploration and to provide a level of comfort when using the Net. Welcome aboard for the first of many exciting travels; keep your guidebooks handy. Teaching and learning will never again be the same.

*Carolyn Markuson*
*President, biblioTECH Corporation*
*Sudbury, Massachusetts*

# Preface ■

The Internet is a key element in reforming public K–12 education.... The Internet's boundless information resources and communications capabilities are not only enlightening but fun.

*Peter Donkers*
*Technology & Distance Education Branch*
*British Columbia Ministry of Education*

**THIS IS A BOOK ABOUT EDUCATIONAL IMPROVEMENT** through strong, contemporary library media development. It is driven by the belief that new, global computing networks require, more than ever, the skills possessed uniquely by educators trained in the information sciences and the helping arts. It asserts that school library media professionals (we use "media librarians" as shorthand) should play key roles in leading schools toward an information-centered curriculum.

Although this is also a book about the burgeoning global accumulation of networked computers called "the Internet," this is not a technical manual. Technical features about the Internet are discussed, but in the context of media librarianship, when such detail illustrates educational power for students and teachers and leadership potential for the library media program. *Readers with no previous networking experience may wish to go straight to chapters 6 and 7 after finishing the first chapter.* These two chapters outline the basics for using common Internet tools. The marketplace is replete with technical information about the Internet. Much of this information resides on the Internet itself (inaccessible, of course, until network fundamentals are mastered).

Because computer networking technology changes by the minute, technical details may be obsolete before a first written draft reaches a printer. Please understand, therefore, that some of the specific Internet information mentioned here may have changed, disappeared, or been superseded by the time you read about it. Don't despair. The larger organizational principles behind this book will better withstand the test of time.

The first chapter of the book discusses the learning environments where networked computers can support teacher growth, promote learning, and enhance the role of the library media program. Here, the history, structure, and future of the Internet are outlined, as is the basic network vocabulary. An overview of leadership potential for media librarians is also included.

Chapter 2 presents ideas for planning the enrichment of schooling through the Internet. In a sense, the entire book should be viewed as an aid to planning; therefore, this second chapter explicitly focuses on the planning process for library media development. Chapter 3 examines the Internet's potential for integrating the community fully and deeply in the life of the school. In this chapter, alternative network scenarios are presented for adaptation in different kinds of school settings.

Chapter 4 examines staff development for media librarians who can—and should— be central in supporting the school's growing use of the Internet. This chapter presents a theoretical foundation for staff development, and then discusses Internet tools and resources that sustain effective staff development in self-renewing schools. The fifth chapter focuses on policy issues raised by Internet integration. Matters such as etiquette, acceptable use, equity, copyright, plagiarism, and the integrity of student research are examined. Again, relevant resources on the Internet are cited so that readers may browse at their leisure.

Chapter 6 offers an in-depth discussion of the newer tools that Internet-using educators will encounter (for example, the World Wide Web and desktop Internet videoconferencing), with guidelines for access and application to the curriculum. Pointers to rich educational resources available with each tool are included. Chapter 7 examines the more traditional Internet tools, such as e-mail, file transfer protocol (FTP), and remote login (Telnet and Gopher).

A glossary of terms deemed significant to the media librarian "travel agent" appears at the end of the book, as do citations for additional resources. These supplement the works cited in each of the chapters. Four appendixes are also offered:

- Appendix A: A pathfinder assignment for Internet-centered staff development

- Appendix B: A sample computer network acceptable use policy from the Nueva School in Hillsborough, California

- Appendix C: A working document on fair use (copyright) from various U.S. library associations

- Appendix D: Guidelines for research citations from Internet sources

As an aid to navigation, floppy disks are provided on the inside back cover of this book. Each disk contains a different version (one for the Macintosh and the other for Windows) of a browsing directory for the World Wide Web. Organized on a chapter-by-chapter basis, a pointer is included for every Web resource cited in the book. Thus, readers may browse the Web as they read about specific sites. With a GUI Web browser (such as Netscape or MOSAIC) running, readers will be able to open their floppy disk files and select hot spots (explained in chapters 1 and 6) that will link them directly to each cited resource. Because many school computers remain unequipped with CD-ROM players, the choice of floppy disks, rather than a CD-ROM, is deliberate. Among the seven chapters, more than 200 Web sites are included.

The disk tool included with this book should help media librarians make a persuasive case for local investment in computer networking. Disk in hand, network advocates can quickly demonstrate the power and utility of Internet resources to administrators, school board members, parents, and community representatives. If the school lacks sufficient network access to run the disk-based HTML file, a demonstration could be scheduled at a local college or university, a networked business, or other resource organization. Be aware, however, that some of the hot spots will have changed between the production of this disk and the time it is used for demonstration.

One of the Internet's greatest strengths is its adaptability to a variety of computer platforms. Whether your networked computer is a Macintosh, an IBM-compatible, or some other platform, it makes little difference to the Internet journey you are about to take.

So, go to your networked computer. Pop in the disk. Open the book. And begin your journey. Bon voyage!

# Acknowledgments ■

**AS THIS BOOK WAS EVOLVING**, several colleagues provided valuable and necessary help. They gave advice, reviewed drafts, contributed passages, and made noteworthy suggestions. Without them, the manuscript would still be residing somewhere between the authors' minds and the editor's desk at Libraries Unlimited. They are listed alphabetically: Charlie Bragg, Dorothy Burke, Ken Cain, Dik Dee, Charlie Friel, Joyce Gibson, Burton Goodrich, Thomas Kane, Mike Lucas, Carolyn Markuson, Maggie Moynihan, Robert Rettew, Linda Setterlund, Mitch Shuldman, and Ann von der Lippe.

Kate Collier designed the World Wide Web navigation tool provided on the disks accompanying this book. Jessie LeBaron created the images on the home page disk files and at the beginning of each chapter. Setting a positive and fitting tone, Carolyn Markuson, president of biblioTECH Corporation, wrote the foreword and contributed sections of chapter 2. To all these people, we are grateful for the "extra miles" contributed beyond the ordinary demands of very busy lives.

Many of the Internet sources cited herein were discovered through the persistence and enthusiasm of the many students who have taken courses or attended workshops offered by the authors. Through focused search strategies and serendipitous happenstance, these students have uncovered countless resources that the authors would never have found on their own.

Time devoted to authoring books is time not spent on other matters. Those "other matters" typically include the people closest to us, with whom shared moments are surely more important than endless sessions at computer keyboards. Our spouses, families, friends, and colleagues have attended to our needs while putting up with the attention we have diverted from theirs. We thank them for their patience.

Finally, we are grateful for David Loertscher's confidence in this project, and for committing Libraries Unlimited to publishing it. Kim Dority, Constance Hardesty, Steve Haenel, and the Libraries Unlimited staff have worked tirelessly to transform a rough work-in-progress into a finished product. They may not appreciate the "friendly midwife" analogy, but that is what they have been.

## Chapter 1 ■

# Leadership, the Internet, and the Library Media Program

How did [our] country come to this? Why, when it's so much cheaper to educate somebody than to keep them in prison, can you get a better library in a prison than in a school?

*President Bill Clinton*
*February 22, 1994*

**A Scenario: Cynthia's Challenges, circa 2020**

Eleventh-grader Cynthia Berkeley winds up two hours of bio-technology research using her personal digital assistant (PDA). This school-supplied portable PDA is connected to the school's information network center, which in turn is connected by high-speed lines to a worldwide array of resources and interactive communication sites. Cynthia has been examining microscopic images of damaged brain cells with her mentor lab technologist at the nearby medical center. Through her hand-held PDA, she can simultaneously communicate with her mentor, tap into microscopic laboratory images, and meet via live videoconference with her teachers, schoolmates, and other skilled resource persons who are collaborating on a research project on Alzheimer's disease prevention.

Several years ago, Cynthia and her peers gave up commuting to school every day. It really wasn't necessary, except when she needed face-to-face interaction with her teachers and student colleagues. When away from school, she is required to log in every hour from another approved work site, such as her town's Public Information Center (formerly called "the Town Library"). At other times, she logs in from the medical center, or works at some alternative curriculum-centered worksite. Earlier today, with her PDA's nano-cam feature, Cynthia conducted a live "video-huddle" with Toshiro, Olga, Jean-Claude, and Samidh, all members of an international work cluster on politics and civil rights. Language was no problem. The PDA translation protocol provided clear voice and text in the language of each user.

Cynthia's PDA has no keyboard. It has a fold-out flat panel screen that offers twenty inches of viewing space. Every PDA function is launched either by voice, by electronic pen, or by mouse.

As she folds up her PDA, Cynthia's thoughts turn to the evening's activity. Using her own home CyberSurfer (or HCS—a consumer-equipped version of her PDA), Cynthia decides to "go" to a virtual music event. Sure, virtuality is no substitute for the real thing, but through a virtuality software plug-in, Cynthia can sample sensory-enhanced music that she could never afford in live concert. Just as she is launching her HCS to access an affordable file on the *Virtual Entertainment Network*, an incoming message overrides her network startup. It is her cyber-challenged dad, saying he is coming home with a new "palmputer" featuring SpeedLINK, a wireless networking device. Dad asks Cynthia to help get it up and running. Darn! There goes the virtual concert! Cynthia's HCS may provide full immersion in musical virtuality, but it *will not* configure her dad's new computer.

# The Internet and Schools: A Potential for Leadership

**CYNTHIA BERKELEY'S FUTURE LIFE IN CYBER SCHOOL** may not emerge exactly as depicted here, but the notion that current educational institutions face revolutionary change is hard to dispute. The technologies driving Cynthia's scenario exist as you read these words. Either schools will respond more nimbly to such technological change than history suggests, or they may be cast aside, unneeded and unsupported, as Lewis Perelman so harshly predicted in 1992. Schools need expertise and leadership to anticipate change and to control the nature of their response.

Honey and McMillan (1993) have pointed out that most teachers cannot access the technology required to use the Internet effectively. Many schools remain inadequately equipped or staffed for widespread network use (Office of Technology Assessment—OTA 1995). Learning to use the Internet can be a challenge. New software tools are making such access infinitely easier for the lay user, but as ease-of-access grows, so does the range of available tools and information sources on the Internet. Barriers of difficulty may therefore be replaced with other constraints, such as network traffic jams and volume over-load. Some educators may shrink from confronting these ever-expanding informational demands. The media librarian can help them maintain their optimism and courage.

Capitalizing on the emergence of powerful computing and interconnected global networks, "virtual libraries" are now emerging from a traditional library foundation. From the collections of the American History Project at the Library of Congress, a World Wide Web (WWW or the Web) site offers an unparalleled array of images and oral histories from the Great Depression, the Civil War, and other eras of this nation's history. These may be found at the following World Wide Web address (chapter 6 offers information on how to access Web sites, and an Internet overview appears later in this chapter):

**http://lcweb2.loc.gov/**

Educators wishing to focus on the scientific contributions of American minorities will find images and information about the history of Afro-American inventions and inventors at the Louisiana State University library at:

**http://www.lib.lsu.edu/lib/chem/display/faces.html**

Focusing on America's European roots, the Deering Library at Northwestern University now provides a searchable collection of over 1,200 digitized images on the Paris Siege and Commune of 1871 (Swanson 1995). This resource is available at:

**http://www.library.nwu.edu:80/spec/siege/**

For those with a more literary turn of mind, Columbia University's Bartleby Project offers on-line resources ranging from the original 1909 edition of *Bartlett's Quotations* to full-text renditions of English writing by such classic authors as Houseman and Yeats. For this, go to:

**http://www.columbia.edu/acis/bartleby/**

Modeled after the recent "Day in the Life of . . ." photojournalist series of books recording commonplace events in several countries, a relatively new Web resource offers an animated, image-rich snapshot of one day's activity (February 8, 1996) on the Internet. This extraordinary document, called *24 Hours in Cyberspace* is not for a quick "hit-and-run" Web visit. For those with the time and interest, though, an hour or more at the following site will be a treat:

**http://www.Cyber24.com/**

These suggestions are but a minuscule smattering of the vast and growing array of cultural, informational, and educational archives on the Web available to learners every-where. Because of their rarity, original documents from any of these sites would otherwise be unavailable. Now, though, they can support the teaching of American and European history and culture worldwide. In this way, libraries become "virtual museums," blurring the functional distinction between these two kinds of cultural organization.

By the same token, teachers now enjoy an abundance of resources, not only on the Web, but also through a variety of electronic communities connecting professionals through distributed e-mail, network bulletin boards, newsgroups, and shared workspace. Resources of this kind are so numerous that no single book could cover all the useful sites for any professional group. This chapter, and chapters 2 through 5, offer selective pointers to resources deemed germane to the topics under discussion.

Setting up Web home pages with links to in-house and external multimedia resources has become quite simple. Schools may now realize the potential for collaborating with historical societies, environmental groups, and public libraries to post unique local resources based on student research for global perusal. Without doubt, the library media program is essential to such information-centered resource sharing.

By education and disposition, media librarians are uniquely endowed to be their schools' Internet "travel agents." More than most other education professionals, media librarians are familiar with electronic information networking and the fundamental principles behind Internet access and use. Possessing experience and expertise with electronic information tools, media librarians are not intimidated by networked computers or by massive volumes of information. They can raise the school's comfort level about the global resource at its doorstep and perform the role of "information cyber-agent."

## The Media Librarian as Leader–Collaborator

**NETWORK DESIGN AND DEVELOPMENT** should be driven by the educational mission of the school. Honey and Henríquez (1993) have found library media specialists to be exceptional telecommunications leaders in their schools, for they know about pedagogy and the information resources that support it. They are uniquely skilled at finding things, helping others find things, and applying information to the goals of teaching and learning. Working with other key school personnel—notably the district or building technology coordinator—media librarians play an essential role in evaluating the relative merits of competing network decisions.

This is where questions of school structure and pedagogical philosophy are so important. Tradition-bound schools will be hard pressed to argue persuasively for network development and Internet access. Scarce resources will already be overcommitted to items that support more traditional practice (such as texts, workbooks, and integrated computer learning [ILS] systems).

Huntley's (1993) distinction between the "constructivist" versus the "instructional" model of network development is useful. Constructivists value pedagogical strategies that promote the construction of student knowledge and the discarding of misconceptions through interaction with peers and tutors (teacher teams, community members, cultural resources, and a rich array of selectively evaluated information sources). Instructionists, in contrast, tend to be more comfortable with the notion of teacher-as-expert/student-as-vessel defined by the simple dynamic of a teacher-to-student flow of knowledge.

Instructionist schools might be attracted to centralized facilities featuring comprehensive ILS files, in which workstation sites would function as client nodes on a system that serves them with a comprehensive menu of prepackaged files for instruction and classroom management. Under such a model, workstations would be concentrated in computer labs rather than distributed among classrooms and other resource areas.

A constructivist philosophy, however, would favor distributed computer networks, in which files are easily exchanged among local workstations and readily exchanged with outside networks. In such a model, software applications and data are shared and used when and where they are needed, and the network is set up to tap a rich array of resources about which judgments are made according to the local dynamics of learning rather than the preconceived values of a systemic software package. This kind of environment suggests a distribution of workstations across the areas where teachers and children work (classrooms, the library/media center, teacher workrooms, counseling areas, and maybe even a computer lab or two).

Media librarians seeking to assist teachers, trainers, and curriculum developers with information on constructivism and curriculum design will find Stephen Sanford's home page of writings and referrals particularly useful. It can be found at:

**http://ouray.cudenver.edu/~slsanfor/**

Through the Internet, Cornell University provides an electronic distribution of papers presented at its annual conference on misconceptions and education in science and math. These works are available from:

**http://132.236.243.68/INDEX2.htm**

Schools are increasingly stressing learning models based on diverse student learning styles (Armstrong 1994; Gardner 1991) and on information resources of the real world. Helpful discussion about the related topic of multiple intelligence learning theory and some of its most prominent proponents, including Howard Gardner, may be found at:

**http://k12.cnidr.org:90/edref.mi.intro.html**

**http://www.greywolf.com/coyote/general/mi.html**

Today's educators confront the challenge of how to prepare students to use the growing profusion of available information. As education changes, there is a push toward resource-centered learning, as opposed to the textbook-based learning of previous years (Haycock 1991). The library media center is the focus of curricular life and a classroom in its own right.

For students to learn how to access, evaluate, and use information, more emphasis on learning processes than outcomes is needed (Eisenberg and Brown 1992). If this is true, media librarians are key to helping teachers integrate effective research into successful classroom practice (Kuhlthau 1989). Such help might conform to Vygotsky's notion of the zone of proximal development (1978), described as "the distance between [a child's] actual developmental level as determined by independent problem-solving and the level of potential development as determined under adult guidance" (131).

The nature of the Internet blends well with a constructivist learning environment for this kind of media librarian intervention. Under proper adult guidance, students are meant to work independently and purposefully, assimilating new information and accommodating existing intellectual frameworks to an expanding knowledge base. A correct assessment of the appropriate zone of intervention (for students and teachers) informs the media librarian about when to step in, and when to step aside, to let learning ride its own momentum.

McKenzie (1994, 3) writes, "enterprising media specialists learn to navigate Internet before anybody else in the school, knowing that they can provide guidance to both students and staff as they tackle this often frustrating information source." Writing about future scenarios for school networking, McKenzie warns of an emerging banking model, where information services are distributed, much as automatic teller machines dispense financial services, without professional assistance. A more benign development would reframe the media librarian role to provide skilled intervention with teachers and students needing to make curricular sense of the new, inchoate electronic information load. He suggests four key media librarian functions on the new cyberturf:

- pilot (lead information consultant for curriculum planning and development)
- information mediator (lead strategist for filtering and evaluating information for effective teaching and learning)
- information technology (IT) manager (lead designer of networks and facilities to access resources most appropriate to the school's curricular mission)
- curator (keeper of sensory artifacts and resources not accessible by electronic means)

Within McKenzie's framework, several more specific opportunities for leadership bear mention. Perhaps as no other school function, the library media program can:

- organize in-school professional development activities related to the Internet
- serve as an information clearinghouse for teachers, administrators, policy makers, parents, and community members
- import, organize, and redistribute information from national or international sources (e.g., color images from space)
- recommend acceptable use policies for access to local networks and the Internet
- coordinate school compliance with copyright and information-ownership guidelines
- structure community access to networks
- develop training and awareness-building strategies for parents and taxpayers
- facilitate the local design of electronic bulletin boards, Gopher menus, and Web home pages

McKenzie's paper[1] on library futures is available at:

### http://www.pacificrim.net/~mckenzie/libraries.html

The Internet's new professional opportunities should encourage the media librarian to keep abreast of the current turbulence in library digitization and the global consolidation of library cataloguing. On the Web, there are many directories of libraries and library-centered public access catalogues (PACs). The grandparent Internet PAC is the Colorado Alliance of Research Libraries (CARL). The CARL Web site offers comprehensive "hot-linked" directories of research, resources, and other catalogues. It is found at:

### http://www.carl.org/

On the strength of its well-organized referrals to other relevant sites, and data on its cutting-edge library digitization project, another "must-visit" Web site is found at the University of California at Berkeley:

**http://sunsite.berkeley.edu/**

Becker (1994) writes about a culture of innovation within certain schools. Technology-using educators feed and draw nourishment from that culture. If it is to survive, however, it needs a critical mass, and it needs to grow. Therefore, the library media program must identify with the school's technology "pioneers." By the same token, it must also serve as a bridge to the "settlers," providing information, training, encouragement, and support.

# What Is the Internet?

**THE INTERNET IS A LOOSE AMALGAM** of individual networks and computer systems, all operating according to agreed-upon network protocols that allow the worldwide transfer of information among systems built on a variety of operating platforms. As distinct from many of the well-known commercial on-line computer networks (e.g., America Online, Compuserv, Prodigy), no individual, company, agency, or institution owns or controls the Internet.

Rooted in the military culture of the cold war, the Internet's original ancestor was established at the Advanced Research Projects Agency (ARPA) of the U.S. Department of Defense. It was called ARPAnet, and was created as a robust, heavily redundant system capable of carrying critical military data throughout a relatively small network of what were then powerful computers. ARPAnet was designed to function properly regardless of any kind of network disruption, no matter how cataclysmic.

The original ARPAnet has been replaced by a succession of bigger, faster, more powerful networked systems, leading to today's Internet. Sensing the potential of distributed computing for science discovery and application, the National Science Foundation created a network dedicated to academic research and development based on the ARPA's Internet Protocol. Operating from a system of regional computing systems interwoven by an Internet "backbone," the Internet offered researchers immediate access to colleagues and files throughout the world.

The Internet is a *distributed* system of interconnected computers and networks. This means that no single hyper-computer or super-network drives it. Rather, it is an enormous, electronic global "neighborhood." Some "houses" are bigger and more luxurious than others, but each sets its own rules and arranges its own furniture.

Because of its federated nature, a democratic Internet user culture has emerged, resulting in an unregulated, sometimes disorganized, collection of universally accessible information. To help users navigate the Internet highway, the Ziff-Davis Publishing Company has published an *Internet Roadmap* (Brisbin et al. 1995, 1996), available both as an interactive on-line resource and in a paper, fold-out, highway map format. At a glance, this attractive fold-out map shows prominent Internet sites organized into subject category zones, and offers a cogent overview of Internet topography. More information is available on the Web at:

**http://www.zdnet.com/macuser/**

# Basic Internet Vocabulary

**THE INTERNET IS BASED ON THE IDEA OF INFORMATION DISTRIBUTION** rather than centralized feeding. Some Internet members operate their own *local area networks*, called *LANs*. (Computer networks ranging across broader territories are called *wide area networks* or *WANs*. No precise boundary distinguishes a LAN from a WAN. If the network is confined to a building, it is probably a LAN; if it covers a whole state or more, it is a WAN. Only the network administrator would know for sure.) LANs that are connected to high-speed telecommunication lines allow many individual workstations to use advanced Internet features simultaneously (see chapter 5). More primitive systems simply allow *terminal emulation*, as though the desktop PC were only a "dumb" video terminal connected to a central host computer.

Any computer directly connected to the Internet is called a *node*. Each node has its own unique address of alphabetic letters separated by dots (see the following). Such an address identifies the member system to other users who need to communicate with it. (Actually, these alphabetical addresses are simply logical, recallable pointers or aliases for the numeric Internet addresses, which are always four sets of numbers, also separated by dots. Nobody is likely to remember the numbers; hence, the substitute system of letters.)

Internet computers are named according to a strict domain system. From left to right, the address letters denote specific-to-general information. For example, "COPERNICUS" in the following sample address denotes the name of the particular internetworked computer or computer cluster. "BBN" signifies the host institution (BOLT, BERANEK and NEWMAN). "COM" shows the kind of institution, or *domain*. The following domains can be found on the Internet:

- COM = commercial firm (e.g., COPERNICUS.BBN.COM)
- EDU = educational institution (e.g., WOODS.UML.EDU)
- GOV = government agency (e.g., ARC.NASA.GOV)
- MIL = military unit (e.g., NIC.DDN.MIL)
- NET = network (e.g., NNSC.NSF.NET)
- ORG = private noncommercial organization (e.g., PAC.CARL.ORG)

Institutions outside the United States are typically identified by two-letter codes at the end of their addresses (e.g., "CA" for Canada, "UK" for United Kingdom). With skyrocketing Internet growth and globalization, many American addresses are now showing "US" as their rightmost domain identifier. Some new American addresses also carry their two-letter state postal code immediately to the left of the "US" designation.

Internet account-holders have *usernames* that identify them as legitimate citizens of an Internet member computer or computing system. Activating a user account is called *login* or *logon*. Closing an interactive session is *logout* or *logoff*. So that the system will know that you are who you say you are, you are issued a confidential *password*. Passwords can be changed by the user; in fact, some networks require passwords to be changed from time to time.

In a distributed system, member computers function as *servers*, *clients*, or both. These terms mean what they say. A server acts as a distribution mechanism for information or as a provider of specialized services such as file storage, high-quality print-ing, or Internet routing. Client computers access servers when they need a particular task performed on their behalf.

To function systematically, a network must operate according to common procedures, or *protocols*. The Internet operates on a protocol system called *TCP/IP* (Transmission Con-trol Protocol/Internet Protocol). Although individual member computers may operate locally on different operating *platforms* (e.g., DOS, Windows, UNIX, Macintosh), the Internet-specific communication operations are common to all and conform to the TCP/IP protocol.

Once you are up and running with some entry-level skill on your own network connec-tion, you can retrieve much more information about the Internet from a variety of Web sites. A good place to start is at the Boston Computer Museum:

**http://www.net.org/is/WhatIsInternet.html**

# What Can Be Accomplished on the Internet?

**ONLY A FEW YEARS AGO,** Internet tools were accessed by a rather arcane set of com-mands. At its most fundamental level, the Internet enables several kinds of operation:

- electronic mail and mailing lists

- remote login (or "Telnet")

- file transfer protocol (FTP)

- newsgroups/bulletin boards

- real time communication, including "chat" and videoconferencing

More recently, user-friendly information services (e.g., Gopher and the World Wide Web) have come to offer simpler ways to provide, locate, or use Internet resources. Newer software tools have emerged to facilitate easier use of e-mail, FTP, Telnet, and Gopher. These are called *graphic user interface* (GUI) tools. Important Internet functions are examined in more detail in chapters 6 and 7, but a brief introduction of the better-known tools follows here.

## *World Wide Web*

The World Wide Web interactively links a vast global aggregation of Internet data that can be accessed simply by choosing highlighted words or phrases on the home page of a Web browser such as Netscape, MOSAIC, Internet Explorer (graphical interface versions), or Lynx (a text-only version). Local home pages can be created for any Internet node. With powerful personal computers and high-speed telecommunication connections, information on the Web can be viewed and captured in any format: ordinary text, image, audio, or motion picture. Older, less powerful computers, or those performing as dumb terminals with dial-up access to a remote Internet node, may be limited to text-only use of the Web.

Although the newer Web browsers are very powerful, they can be made even more powerful with a variety of *plug-ins*, *helper applications*, and *applets*. These tools are soft-ware applications that enable the Web traveler to view and create certain files formatted in special ways that cannot be managed by the browser software alone.

One such tool is RealAudio, a plug-in that enables a user to hear files formatted in sound, such as some of the NPR Radio files. Another is Java, an applet that supports a variety of fancy home page features, such as scrolling text, three-dimensional images, or animated graphics. Many of these helper applications can be downloaded on the Web. Once configured with your browser software, they launch automatically whenever your browsing finds a file featuring such an application. Java, developed by Sun Microsystems, Inc., may be downloaded from:

**http://java.sun.com/**

## Gopher

Gopher applications have proliferated on the Internet, but are now being eclipsed by the Web. Gopher servers are now available worldwide, creating logical and transparent mechanisms for finding and retrieving many Internet resources. A Gopher server will organize the presentation of the host institution's resources in a series of directories and subdirectories, some of which are indexed for keyword searches using search tools such as Veronica.

## E-mail and Mailing Lists

Most individuals with access to an Internet-connected computer or computing system have an e-mail address, and therefore can exchange private mail quickly with any other addressee. Many Internet users, however, use e-mail for purposes other than one-on-one private correspondence. They may subscribe to one or more of many public e-mail distribution lists, sometimes called *listservs*, *mailservs*, or *majordomos*. Members of these electronic mail distribution lists make up virtual communities of interest related to individual need.

## Newsgroups/Bulletin Boards

Newsgroups serve as discussion forums for people interested in a wide variety of topics. As distinct from e-mail lists, newsgroup users may read, post, reply to, and follow up on newsgroup messages without their own personal subscriptions. Several newsgroups are inappropriate for use by schoolchildren. Media librarian leadership can help formulate local practices and policies for acceptable use in schools. This issue is discussed thoroughly in chapter 5.

## Interactive Chat

Users impatient with waiting for responses to e-mail messages may use the Internet "talk" tool with other users in real time. On some nodes, one-on-one on-screen "phone" conversations may be launched with other users who happen to be logged on at another Internet site when the call is made. On a broader scale, users may join a variety of Internet chat groups, in which several connected users converse interactively at the same time. Like newsgroups, conversations in some of these "chat rooms" may be mindless, offensive, or harmful. Internet Relay Chat (IRC), the tool for on-screen group discussion, is disabled on some local Internet nodes. Educators should treat these tools with care, especially when children are involved.

## Telnet

Telnet (or remote login) enables users to log in to Internet computers other than their own. Thus, they may make use of publicly available resources throughout the world. Some of the available Telnet resources are invaluable for educators. Globetrotters often find Telnet a boon. With temporary access to any Internet host in the world, travelers may Telnet home to their host computers and conduct work just as they would at their own desks.

## FTP

File Transfer Protocol (FTP) allows Internet-connected computers to send and receive computer data as complete files. Many publishers, researchers, and software developers have established anonymous FTP sites where documents, fully formatted applications, and multimedia files are catalogued and stored for access by other Internet users. Public FTP sites may be searched using a *search engine* called Archie.

## Search Tools

Resources on the Internet are getting easier to find. Nonetheless, skilled librarianship is a distinct asset to any Internet-using school community. Different Internet tools require unique search procedures. The Web, for example, features several search engines, each with its own search scope, procedures, directories, and indexes. These individual engines have spawned newer meta-tools that run simultaneous searches of several engines in a single operation. An example is MetaCrawler at:

**http://metacrawler.cs.washington.edu/**

Gopher and FTP feature their own unique search tools. Throughout Internet history, finding its individual users has been a special challenge. Newer Internet "people directories," such as

**http://www.whowhere.com/**

are yielding better, but not infallible, results. More detailed information on Internet searching appears in chapters 6 and 7, in the discussion of the corresponding Internet tools.

## Internet Videoconferencing

Low-cost Internet videoconferencing is now possible on the Internet. A popular, public-domain videoconferencing tool is *CU-SeeMe* (pronounced "see you, see me"), developed at Cornell University. Electronically shared work is becoming more commonplace as Internet computing capacity expands along with access to the global infrastructure. Because of variations in Internet computing capacity and access bandwidth, these relatively advanced applications are not yet universally accessible. Some of the newer Internet tools enable transparent access to many older tools. For example, remote files can be transferred and Telnet connections made through a Web browser or through Gopher.

With sound- and video-processing network software, the Internet is carrying increasing volumes of audio programming. "Internet radio" is a growing phenomenon. Media librarians might be particularly interested in the program archives of National Public Radio, available at:

**http://www.npr.org/**

With the use of network audio player software, current and archived NPR features can be heard through a computer's loudspeaker system. Such software may be downloaded free of charge from:

**http://www.realaudio.com/**

Be warned, though: the more complex the medium, the larger the file that contains it. Video files, for example, are enormous and will take hours to download over ordinary phone lines with even the speediest conventional modems. Older desktop computers with low internal memory capacity (RAM), or with small hard disks, may not be able to download them at all.

## Internet Growth: From Trickle to Tsunami

**ONE OF SEVERAL TIMELINES FOR THE INTERNET,** *Hobbes' Internet Timeline* (Zakon 1996) is available on the Web at:

**http://info.isoc.org/guest/zakon/Internet/History/HIT.html**

or by e-mail request to:

**timeline@hobbes.mitre.org**

It traces the origin of the Internet back to the sense of shock among American scientists and politicians caused in 1957 by the launch of Russia's first-ever space orbiting satellite, *Sputnik*. The earliest Internet operation began in 1969. Then, the Internet comprised four hosts (UCLA, Stanford, UCSB, and the University of Utah). At mid-life (1982), the Internet had grown to approximately 250 hosts. By 1996, there were almost 10 million hosts. The list of hosts continues to grow explosively.

Approximately 150 countries, on an ever-growing list, are directly connected to the Internet. When we add other networks capable of interfacing with the Internet in some manner or other, the number of nations rises to more than 200 (Internet Society 1995). In 1995, the number of WWW home pages was growing 20 percent per month (Howley 1995). This means one new home page roughly every fifteen minutes! Adapted from Zakon's work (1996), some noteworthy Internet benchmarks are illustrated in figure 1.1.

The numbers in the charts in figures 1.2 through 1.4 are based on Peterson's Quality Education Data (1995). The Internet has clearly become a forceful presence in schools. Figure 1.2 shows the status of school Internet access in 1994, and figure 1.3 indicates heavy school preference for the Internet over other on-line network services.

Among Internet-using schools, some are connected directly through a commercial Internet service provider, some through access to a nearby college or university, others through a statewide public service network, and still others through an intermediate service unit or a formal collaboration among several districts.

Computer networking has grown at all schooling levels between 1991 and 1995, apparently at a slower rate than in society at large. Figure 1.4 shows growth in local area networks during this period.

The news from QED is not incontestably positive. Not surprisingly, computer access for minorities and for low-income school districts lags behind that of more affluent districts, and the gap is not closing. As public schools struggle to overcome the problem of teacher access—identified by the OTA and others—the disparity between today's leading schools and their less advantaged counterparts will surely continue to challenge educators

**Figure 1.1   Major Internet benchmarks**
*Adapted from Zakon (1996). Reprinted with permission. To retrieve the most recent version of the time line, go to* http://info.isoc.org/guest/zakon/Internet/History/HIT.html

and public decision makers. (The question of technology equity is addressed more fully in chapter 5.)

At this writing, QED data and charts are available on-line at the following Web site:

**http://www.edshow.com/QED/**

# Connecting to the Internet

**MAKING THE CASE** for school networking is a document prepared for the California Department of Education (Maak, Carlitz, and Rutkowski 1995). This whole file is available at:

**http://goldmine.cde.ca.gov/WWW/Technology/K-12/benefit_paper.html**

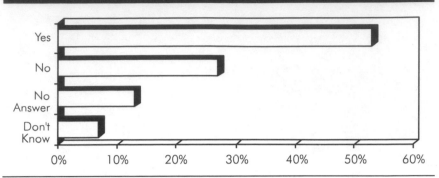

**Figure 1.2   Districts showing at least one school using the Internet in 1993–1994**
*Used with permission of Quality Education Data, a division of Peterson's © 1995.*

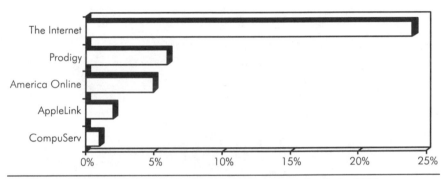

**Figure 1.3   Comparison of on-line services used by schools in 1994**
*Used with permission of Quality Education Data, a division of Peterson's © 1995.*

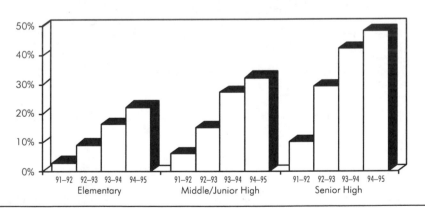

**Figure 1.4   LAN growth in public schools by grade level, 1991–1995**
*Used with permission of Quality Education Data, a division of Peterson's © 1995.*

The authors suggest that networking addresses three major issues for schools:

- equity (as networking assumes ever-greater importance as a means of information transfer)

- isolation (encouraging global peer interaction and collaboration for teachers and students in a manner that approximates the realities of work in a twenty-first-century economy)

- educational reform (encouraging constructivist teaching and improved access to professional development resources)

They conclude by saying, "School networking applications support teaching and learning strategies which cultivate professional and academic excellence and prepare individuals for a life of learning and productive employment" (6).

Many models exist for connecting schools to the Internet. As a simple approach, schools can equip a single personal computer with a standard modem and provide that computer with access to the outside world through a conventional telephone line. Such access might be dedicated to telecomputing, or the phone line might support other traffic as well, such as voice or fax. Because only one interactive network session at a time is possible through such an arrangement, the constraint on instructional use—even in the smallest schools—is severe. The slower the modem, the greater the constraint.

A more satisfactory model equips a school with its own internal local area network, including one computer that functions as a router and network server, in turn connected to a higher-capacity dedicated data line (at least 56 kilobits per second) tied directly to an Internet host. With the use of a router or a modem bank instead of a single modem, multiple interactive sessions can be undertaken from different locations within a school building at the same time, and the constraints on instructional and personal use are dramatically relieved.

Satisfaction has its costs, however. Locally networked facilities require significant investment in equipment, software, and personnel. Then there is the cost of wiring the building (often difficult in older structures). Annual telecommunication costs of dedicated high-capacity lines will be greater than shared access to the school's existing voice tele phone system. Finally, networks require regular maintenance, implying a need for skilled technical personnel, and budgetary provision for maintenance and upgrading.

In designing school networks, future needs should be considered. As more powerful applications (using a variety of media, including graphic images, audio, motion video, and real-time videoconferencing) are added, telecommunication bandwidth needs will increase. More—and more powerful—workstations will be needed. Investing in as much bandwidth as possible when a LAN is being installed might avoid undue cost and disruption later on. The text below provides a useful analogy for the technical choices that confront schools.

> As water is supplied to your home through a pipe, data is supplied through a cable to your computer....
> Data cabling [and] water pipes follow some basic rules. Larger pipes are more expensive and have higher support costs than smaller pipes. If you have a swimming pool you know it would be convenient to have a fire hydrant sized pipe available when it comes time to fill

the pool. The swimming pool is like a very large program or application. Sinks, buckets, and water glasses are various size applications. Each application takes a specific amount of time to fill (load) from a water tap. The only way the task of filling various applications can be reduced is to provide more flow capacity (more or larger pipes) to the application.

In the computer environment, movies and digital video programs are equivalent to swimming pools while word processing or text documents are like filling a water glass. Some people are willing to wait the long time necessary to fill the pool with a garden hose and other people are willing to hire the local fire department to pump the water into the pool. The consideration remains cost versus time: does the wait justify the cost savings? The same principle applies to the movement of data throughout local area networks and between networks. If you want to move the data faster, it will cost more. This is where costs to performance ratios are required to optimize performance and balance user requirements against costs.

*Extracted from Thomas E. Scott,* Going Beyond Your Local Area Network. *Paper developed for the California Department of Education, K–12 Network Planning Unit, 1995, available at:*

**http://goldmine.cde.ca.gov/ WWW/Technology/K-12/ISDN.html**

Several resources exist in print and on-line to help the uninitiated media librarian consider the complexities of computer networking in schools. One of these is the ERIC publication *An Educator's Guide to Electronic Networking: Creating Virtual Communities*, by Kurshan, Harrington, and Milbury (1994). In a policy context, Priest (1995) discusses the comparative advantages and costs of several school networking options. Priest's insights reside at the following Web address:

**http://interact.uoregon.edu/MediaLit/FA/MLArticleFolder/cost**

Another perspective on Priest's policy discussion is a work by Carnegie Mellon University's Jon Peha, available at:

**http://www.ece.cmu.edu/afs/ece.cmu.edu/usr/peha/k12**

More powerful telecomputing can be anticipated soon. The federal government has committed itself to expanding the National Information Infrastructure (NII). National and regional telephone utilities are either fighting or merging with cable television companies to participate fully in the development of the information "superhighway." In early 1996, US West, a regional Bell company, acquired Continental Cablevision, one of the nation's major cable television operators. Corporate mergers are forming and falling apart in an intense period of competitive jockeying. Governments puzzle over their potential roles.

How can government ensure that the [emerging] information market-place ... will permit everyone to be able to compete with everyone else for the opportunity to provide any service to all willing customers... ? How can we ensure that it fulfills the enormous promise of education, economic growth and job creation?

It was in this spirit that [President] Clinton and I ... set as a vital national goal linking every classroom in every school in the United States to the National Information Infrastructure. It was in this same spirit that ... I pointed out that when it comes to telecommunications services, schools are the most impoverished institutions in society. And so I was pleased to hear that some companies participating in the communications revolution are now talking about voluntarily linking every classroom in their service areas to the NII.

*From an address by Vice President Al Gore to the Television Academy, January 11, 1994 (from CoSNDISC e-mail list).*

Reinforcing the corporate community's drive to build, and sell access to, a mighty new NII is the commitment of several states to develop powerful, distributed telecommunication networks to support instruction, financial management, administration, and reporting among all their schools. Computer networking is one of the nation's hottest contemporary educational topics, clearly offering a window of opportunity for media librarian leadership.

For schools just getting ready to take their first Internet steps, subscription to a commercial Internet service provider (ISP) with a single-line conventional telephone access might be a good place to start. However, because this kind of service will preclude the critical mass of access needed for meaningful curricular change, such a measure should be considered useful for trial purposes only. With modems rated at 14,400 bits per second (bps) or higher, most GUI interfaces can be used to reasonably good effect. Choosing the right ISP can be a challenge. Each one seems to have its own unique features and pricing structure. Service quality varies dramatically. Help is available, though, from friends and colleagues who have already signed on with an ISP, or from Mecklermedia's national directory of ISPs at the following Web site:

**http://thelist.com/**

Newer, better, faster facilities for hooking into the Internet are on the way, even for rural areas or poorly served locations. Global network data flows of the future promise exponentially faster download times for densely packed, media-rich files (Bray 1996). Consider a moderately dense file of three megabytes containing a modest presentation of text, still images, sound, and a short video clip. The following chart shows how much time varying bandwidths would take to download this file, under ideal conditions, from a server to a client.

| Type of Carrier | Transmission Device | Download Time (3 mb) |
|---|---|---|
| Ordinary voice phone line | 2,400 bps analog modem | 2.5 hours |
| Ordinary voice phone line | 14.4 kbps analog modem | 21 minutes |
| Ordinary voice phone line | 28.8 kbps analog modem | 10.5 minutes |
| Digital ISDN phone line | 128 kbps digital modem | 3.5 minutes |
| Cable TV connection | 10 mbps digital modem | 2.5 seconds |

These approximate download times assume that every network way station between the file source and the download site is working at full capacity, which is rarely true, especially when ordinary voice-grade telephone lines are used. ISDN service is not universally available, and it is not cheap. The ultra-high-speed Internet connections promised via cable television remain a good distance away for most users. Most current cable television systems are not yet configured for computer networking. The optimistic transmission rates promised for this service are based on moderate traffic volumes. Like any road system, heavy volume can slow traffic to a crawl, even on a sixteen-lane superhighway.

Although the arrival time for these newer services cannot be predicted with certainty, their inevitability is beyond dispute. New transmission schemes—wired and wireless—are combining with more powerful data compression tools to assure ever-increasing cyber speed limits.

## Final Words

**OVER THE YEARS,** a distinct culture established itself in the Internet's educational and research community. Perhaps this is due to the noncommercial, noncompetitive nature of people whose primary motivation is to share, rather than control, information. An example is shown in the following expression of gratitude from a member of the LM_Net listserv who had posted a question to the list.

```
Date:     Thu, 27 Jul 1995 13:49:55 -0400
Sender:   School Library Media & Network Communications
          <LM_NET@LISTSERV.SYR.EDU>
From:     Sophia Smith <sosmith@CELLO.GINA.CALSTATE.EDU>
Subject:  Thanks for "Light in the Forest."
To:       Multiple recipients of list LM_NET
          <LM_NET@LISTSERV.SYR.EDU>

Dear LM-Netters,
    What a great response to my query. It was incredible
not only in the detail but also the speed with which I
received the information. This has to be one of the best
listservs on the Internet. I can't begin to thank you
enough.

Sophia
```

Many telecomputing veterans follow a common set of courtesies, often called *netiquette.* The survival of this culture depends on widespread observance of these protocols, which are coming under increasing pressure with the huge expansion of commerce on the Internet.

Information posted on the Internet enters a public domain. All public postings, whether or not they carry a copyright © notice, enter a crowded marketplace over which there is very little control. School colleagues should be informed of this phenomenon. If they cannot tolerate their work being copied or used without their authorization, they should store it only on personal, not networked, storage devices.

The media librarian shares responsibility for network security with other stakeholders (teachers, administrators, network administrators, students, parents). Certain administrative data, such as student assessment results or media circulation data, must remain restricted. Students are entitled to some privacy in their electronic communications but, when networking in their schools, they are using school resources for which educators are responsible. By serving as the clearinghouse for electronic and traditional research on these matters, media librarians can play a critical and judicious role in setting policy and assuring appropriate use.

The volume of Internet information is overwhelming, a condition that will only become more severe in time. This is why intelligent, skilled information searching is so important. By searching, sifting, assisting, and selectively disseminating user-specific resources, media librarians can become school agents for making sense of what might otherwise appear as a torrent of network babble.

Some Internet traffic might offend a teacher or exploit a child. Because it is difficult to balance the librarian's professional aversion to censorship with the natural instinct to create safe learning environments, schools must take particular care to manage the participation of its users (students, teachers, administrators, board members, parents) wisely. The skilled media librarian is well positioned to make judicious recommendations about acceptable use policy and practice.

Internet users need to protect their local systems from the unfortunate but inevitable vandalism that periodically invades connected computers. (See chapter 5 for more discussion of this problem.) With or without premeditated malice, destructive computer "viruses" and "worms" can wreak havoc on unsuspecting victims. Therefore, all imported files should be checked with a current version of an effective virus-checker before local use. Confusing the issue is the fact that some virus alerts showing up on listservs and electronic newsgroups turn out to be hoaxes. A more reliable information source about network-transmitted viruses can be found at Symantec's Antivirus Center:

**http://www.symantec.com/avcenter/**

In this chapter, we have confined our discussion to finding and using Internet resources, and to the media librarian's constructive role as Internet travel agent for the school. Of course, traffic can flow in several directions simultaneously. As you, your colleagues, and your students become Internet-empowered, you may develop an incentive to post local information on the Internet for worldwide audiences. Your school may set up a Web home page. It is not hard to do, and it can be great fun. It offers a powerful public forum for the productive work of students and teachers.

As you become more familiar with Internet navigation, telecomputing becomes second nature, and your initial stumbling will be transformed into an effortless flow. Before you know it, you are maneuvering smoothly through Gopher tunnels and Web sites. As this happens, you enhance your capacity to serve as chief navigator for your educational peers.

# Notes

1. Jamie McKenzie, Director of Libraries, Media, and Technology for the Bellingham, Washington, Public Schools, offers an array of helpful papers about Internet integration in the schools. Some of his additional contributions, with topics and URLs, are:

Technology Connections for Schools:
http://www.pacificrim.net/~mckenzie/cyber.html

Net Researching Skills: Grazing the Net Part 1 & 2:
http//www.pacificrim.net/~mckenzie/grazing1.html

Internet Resources:
http://www.pacificrim.net/~mckenzie/internet.html

See chapters 2 and 5 for additional references to McKenzie's work.

# References

Armstrong, T. 1994. *Multiple intelligences in the classroom.* Alexandria, Va.: Association for Supervision and Curriculum Development.

Becker, H. J. 1994. "How exemplary computer-using teachers differ from other teachers: Implications for realizing the potential of computers in schools." *Journal of Research on Computing in Education* 26(3): 291–321.

Bray, H. 1996. "Watson, come here. I'm stuck downloading." *Boston Sunday Globe*, 3 March.

Brisbin, S., J. Snell, G. Duncan, D. Dempsey, and K. D. Clark. 1995, 1996. *MacUser Internet road map.* New York: Ziff-Davis.

Eisenberg, M. B., and M. K. Brown. 1992. "Current themes regarding library and information skills instruction: Research supporting and research lacking." *School Library Media Quarterly*, 20(2): 103–10.

Gardner, H. 1991. *The unschooled mind: How children think and how schools should teach.* New York: Basic Books.

Gore, A. 1994. Address to the Television Academy, 11 January 1994. Internet e-mail received from CoSNDISC List.

Haycock, C. A. 1991. "Resource-based learning: A shift in the roles of teacher, learner." *NASSP Bulletin* 75(535): 15–21.

Honey, M., and A. Henríquez. 1993. *Telecommunications and K-12 educators: Findings from a national survey.* Educational Resources Information Center. ED 359 923.

Honey, M., and K. McMillan. 1993. *Case studies of K–12 educators' use of the Internet: Exploring the relationship between metaphor and practice.* Educational Resources Information Center. ED 372 726.

Howley, K. 1995. "Buying and selling properties in cyberspace." *Boston Globe*, 22 July.

Huntley, M. 1993. Remarks made at the Annual Retreat of Massachusetts Computer-Using Educators, 14 May 1993. Sandwich, Mass.

Internet Society. 1995. *Global and country top level domains of the world* [on-line]. Available WWW: http://info.isoc.org/
Path: adopsec/
File: index.html

Kuhlthau, C. C. 1989. "Information search process: A summary of research and implications for school library media programs." *School Library Media Quarterly* 18(1): 19–25.

Kurshan, B. L., M. A. W. Harrington, and P. G. Milbury. 1994. *An educator's guide to electronic networking: Creating virtual communities.* Syracuse, N.Y.: ERIC Clearinghouse on Information & Technology.

Maak, L., R. Carlitz, and K. Rutkowski. 1995. *Benefits of school networking* [on-line]. Sacramento, Calif.: California Department of Education.
Available WWW: **http://goldmine.cde.ca.gov/**
Path: **WWW/Technology/K-12/**
File: **benefit_paper.html**

McKenzie, J. 1994. *Libraries of the future* [on-line].
Available WWW: **http://www.pacificrim.net/**
Path: **~mckenzie/**
File: **libraries.html**

Office of Technology Assessment, U.S. Congress. 1995. *Teachers & teaching: Making the connection.* Washington, D.C.: U.S. Government Printing Office.

Peha, J. M. 1995. *Computer Networks in K-12 education* [on-line].
Available WWW: **http://www.ece.cmu.edu/**
Path: **afs/ece.cmu.edu/usr/peha/**
File: **k12**

Perelman, L. J. 1992. *School's out: Hyperlearning, the new technology, and the end of education.* New York: William Morrow.

Priest, W. C. 1995. *Cost-effective networking of schools and homes* [on-line].
Available WWW: **http://interact.uoregon.edu/**
Path: **MediaLit/FA/MLArticleFolder/**
File: **cost**

Quality Education Data. 1995. *Charts and graphs showing technology implementation in American schools* [on-line].
Available WWW: **http://www.odohow.com/**
Path: **QED/**

Scott, T. E. 1995. *Going beyond your local area network* [on-line]. Sacramento, Calif.: California Department of Education.
Available WWW: **http://goldmine.cde.ca.gov/**
Path: **WWW/Technology/K-12/**
File: **ISDN.html**

Swanson, S. 1995. "Libraries go electronic." *Boston Globe*, 6 August.

Vygotsky, L. 1978. *Mind in society: The development of higher psychological processes.* Cambridge, Mass.: Harvard University Press.

Zakon, R. H. 1996. *Hobbes' Internet timeline 2.4a* [on-line].
Available WWW: **http://info.isoc.org/**
Path: **guest/zakon/Internet/History/**
File: **HIT.html**

# Chapter 2

# Planning: The Foundation for Leadership

The great heroes of history are not those who won wars, but those who prevented wars from occurring. History does not record their names for it is blind to uncommitted evils.

*David Pratt (1994)*

Any organization flounders aimlessly without a plan. Planning sets program performance goals and evaluation criteria. It guides the activities and relationships among personnel. If done effectively, it establishes a shared vision of what an organization ought to be doing and how it will carry out its mission. It establishes the foundation for effective public relations. No less than other administrative personnel, school media librarians need to develop and apply effective planning skills. Accordingly, this chapter discusses strategies to plan for school Internet development from a library media perspective.

Planning for Internet integration with the school curriculum presents an intriguing set of questions for the library media program. To nurture effective Internet use, media librarians require a working knowledge of many fields, some of which might not have been part of—or even germane to—their formal professional training. Paramount among these are the capacity to assess institutional needs and the ability to find solutions to identified challenges. Allies will be needed to build and carry out plans in school settings. MacDonald (1995) writes, "Essential to the success of any media center service is support from school administrators, teachers, and the media center committee. Work with these shareholders to develop specific goals for the use of technology, including the Internet, in the media center" (266).

Although this chapter is written from the perspective of a districtwide library media program overseeing school-based centers, countless other models exist. Some school-based programs are very small. Others are staffed by only a part-time librarian. Some school programs have no districtwide oversight. In the on-line document, *Technology Planning for Libraries*, Hockersmith (1994) suggests that effective technology planning by the media librarian requires access to a constantly changing array of resources. Mastraccio's (1995) companion guide, *Technology Planning for Schools*, points exhaustively to such an array from traditional and electronic sources (e.g., Internet sites, ERIC documents, journals, printed reports). These and several other valuable documents are available through the AskERIC Gopher under the subdirectory

### Alphabetical_List_of_InfoGuides:

### Gopher://ericir.syr.edu:70/11/InfoGuides/

Cohen (1994) addresses technology planning from the perspective of library facilities development. Eisenberg and Brown (1992) discuss planning in the context of developing professional skills. Technology planning must examine several additional areas of operation, as outlined here. (Related book chapters are indicated in parentheses.)

- coalition building (this chapter)
- community outreach (chapter 3)
- curriculum development and integration (chapters 3, 6, and 7)
- ethics, privacy, and acceptable use (chapter 5)
- network design and information systems coordination (chapters 1, 3, and 6)
- promotion and publicity (chapters 1, 3, and 4)
- staff development, training, and support (chapter 4)

In a sense, this entire book is an aid to effective planning. However, this chapter explicitly focuses on the planning process.

## Planning Guides: Finding What's Out There

**IN RECENT YEARS,** leaders in the library media and educational technology fields have developed a variety of planning guides for integrating technology and computer networking into various aspects of school life. Some of these guides are centered on infrastructure development; others focus more on curricular infusion, organizational development, or information management. One highly regarded work, *The Switched-On Classroom* (1994), produced by the Massachusetts Software Council, is a step-by-step school technology planning guide. It covers such topics as team building, needs assessment, funding, staff development, program evaluation, and planning for the future. Information about this guide is available on the Internet from the Massachusetts Software Council's Web site. The printed and bound version may be ordered on-line from:

**http://www.swcouncil.org/**

For Massachusetts educators, it may be downloaded without charge from:

**http://www.swcouncil.org/switch2.html**

Because planning guides of this nature have varied emphases and strengths, media librarians may employ different Internet search strategies to locate works particularly germane to their needs. For example, the authors recently posted the following query to the Coalition for School Networking (CoSN) listserv (**cosndisc@yukon.cren.org**) and to LM_Net (**LM_NET@listserv. syr.edu**):

> [We are] interested in finding planning guidelines for school network and technology development in K-12 environments [such as] quality sources available on the Web, on Gopher, or via anonymous FTP. Thanks in advance for whatever ideas you come up with.

Within forty-eight hours of each request, sixteen responses with thirty suggestions were produced, most of them on target and helpful.[1] Some led to specific resources. Others suggested Veronica searches on Gopher, an ERIC search at:

**· http://ericir.syr.edu/Eric**

or at:

**gopher://ericir.syr.edu:70/11/Database**

or a focused Web search using a variety of Web search engines such as WebCrawler at:

**http://webcrawler.com/**

or one of the newer "meta tools" that scan more than twenty search engines at once, such as Savvy at:

**http://savvy.cs.colostate.edu:2000/**

Other rich information sources for planning are listed at the end of this chapter.

# Kinds of Planning

**TWO BROAD KINDS OF PLANNING** are often discussed in the relevant literature: strategic and operational. Both of these are germane to effective library media program development.

The strategic plan establishes a fundamental organizational tone, painting by broad strokes the program's business and informing staff why they are doing what they do. The operational plan, in contrast, is a more detailed accounting of specific organizational goals, often described on a year-to-year basis, with key activities identifying what will be done to meet the goals, by whom, and in what staffing configurations. Operational plans generate program output statements. These outputs describe what conditions will exist at some determined future moment as a result of implementation of the operational plan.

All planning eventually flows to a budget. The program budget defines how an organization's resources will be allocated for achievement of the various planning goals.

Planners need to be flexible, avoiding fixed canons about planning and instead finding approaches that are appropriate to the cultures and missions of their own organizational environments. Dede (1993) warns educational technology planners of the escalating speed of change, not only in technology as such, but also (sometimes as a result of technology) in the surrounding environment. Lorange and Vancil (1977) describe a common set of strategic planning issues, but they caution that universal prescriptions are not appropriate for the unique needs of particular organizations.

Schools, for example, will employ a different process than government units or private businesses. Just as Becker (1994) points out for schools, Deal and Kennedy (1982) indicate that distinct organizational cultures reign in the corporate world. These cultures will influence planning in different ways. Through all kinds of planning, however, important themes recur.

# Elements of Planning

WRITING ABOUT ORGANIZATIONAL PLANNING in the public sector, Jensen (1982) outlined the following six-element operational planning process:

- definition (or redefinition) of the core mission/vision statement

- outline of current program conditions

- assessment of needs and scan of current program conditions

- description of improved program conditions (plan output)

- delineation of key accomplishments related to program improvement

- listing of key decisions related to program improvement

Media librarians might think of strategic and operational planning as two parts of an overall process. The operational plan is developed and implemented over a defined time period and moves forward from the measured results of the previous operational plan. The strategic plan, however, is revisited and refined as necessary. Because an up-to-date strategic plan is an absolute prerequisite to the annual operational plan, it needs review at least as often as the operational plan is developed. In planning for integration of the Internet into the life of the school, then, a library media program might employ its own six-stage process, combining strategic with operational planning techniques:

- designing the planning process (strategic/operational)

- creating or redefining the core mission statement (strategic)

- assessing program needs based on a scan of internal and external environments (strategic/operational)

- describing desired program goals and outputs (operational)

- defining key inputs (tasks) required for desired program outputs (operational)

- assigning responsibilities to key management and program personnel (operational)

Each of these stages is discussed in greater detail later in this chapter.

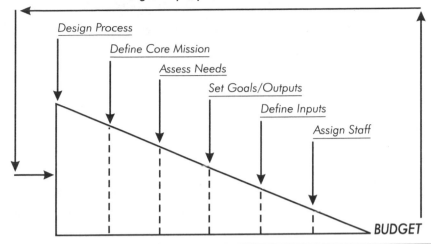

A progressively narrowing planning process:
- Planning leads to budgets
- Budgets adjust plans

Design Process
Define Core Mission
Assess Needs
Set Goals/Outputs
Define Inputs
Assign Staff
BUDGET

**Figure 2.1    The planning process**

Note that budgeting is not itemized as a discrete planning step. The first-prize winner in *Electronic Learning*'s 1995 National Technology Planning Contest, for example, bypassed budgeting in its initial planning process (Ocasio, Gray, and Palazzo 1995). Although budgeting and planning are intimately connected, planning experts are correct in arguing that budgeting is a consequence, rather than a driver, of good planning (see figure 2.1).

Educational program directors sometimes budget by making annual adjustments to their program budget lines. Such a practice only reinforces a tedious recycling of timeworn activity, and renders creative planning virtually impossible.

A good plan requires quantitative, measurable criteria. Good plans are commitments to organizational productivity in terms that combine vision with operational detail. Achievement of such productivity is the promise of the program manager. Even the mission statement should be written in a manner that leads to quantification in the plan's more detailed sections, where the implications for implementation are indicated in light of the program's overall mission.

# Effective Planning Depends on a Good Planning Process

## A Shared Process

Planners (MacDonald 1995; McKenzie 1993, 1994a) often cite the benefits of stakeholder participation in the planning process. *Participation*, however, does not necessarily mean that every stakeholder's private vision becomes a part of the organization's overall vision. It means that key persons are provided a genuine opportunity to influence the final shape of that vision. There should be a visible process for gathering staff "vision inputs" and for communicating how these inputs will aid in shaping organizational goals and mission statements. Jamie McKenzie's papers on planning concepts and on staff development at the following two WWW locations offer helpful guidance:

**http://www.pacificrim.net/~mckenzie/staffd.html**

**http://www.pacificrim.net/~mckenzie/criteria.html**

Shared values shape program targets and generate individual commitments to meeting those targets. Moreover, team members bring different perspectives, expertise, and resources to the planning process. With proper team leadership and staff coordination, team members can be assigned to subcommittees to pursue specialized planning aspects in the context of the organizational vision, the technology goals, and the overall work of the whole team.

In addition to library media staff and school personnel, other significant constituent groups—students, teachers, administrators, parents, and community representatives—should also contribute to the planning process (see remarks on needs assessment later in this chapter). For this reason, library media directors may see fit to establish Internet planning committees and subcommittees whose members contribute the knowledge of the constituencies they represent.

### General Planning Versus Program Planning

Media librarians contribute to educational planning in different ways. They contribute informational resources to the district's (or the school's) overall educational plan, and they plan at the library media program level for the activities falling under their own direct purview. At district and school building levels, media librarians should be equal partners in the educational planning team. At the program level, planning should be informed and guided by curricular missions and goals of the districts and schools served by the library media center. Describing the Madison, Connecticut, district plan, media/technology consultant Bob Hale was quoted as saying, "It's a strategic plan for the district, not just a technology plan" (Ocasio, Gray, and Palazzo 1995: 32).

The planning relationships between library media programs and the districts or schools they serve are depicted in figure 2.2.

This figure shows a dual-triangle planning structure wherein the whole organization's top management provides and receives necessary program data. The smaller triangle (in reality one of several) resting inside the larger one represents the library media program. Planning at the program level can be viewed as a micro-procedure, not only dedicated to its particular program needs, but also contributing to the overall district's planning process. By the same token, district-level planning informs and assists a parallel process at the building level. The main key to success for such a process is a participatory flow of information from the top through the organization's various programs to the grass roots and back up to the top again.

## Creating the Core Mission Statement

**ACCORDING TO CHANDLER** (1994), "A key attribute of knowing where an organization is headed ... involves beginning with the end in mind. An organization's mission statement helps to assure that the end is always kept in mind." The core mission statement articulates the fundamental reason for an organization's existence. Though meant to provide the

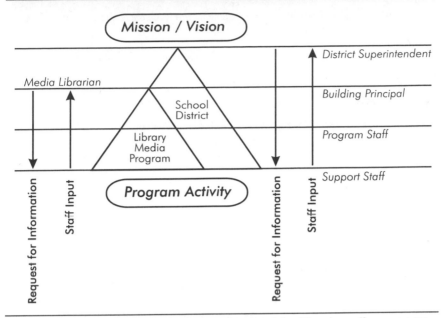

**Figure 2.2   School-district planning environment for library media programs**

foundation for more detailed planning activity, core missions need constant re-examination. *Information Power* (AACL/AECT 1988) suggests the following general mission statement for all school library media programs: "to ensure that students and staff are effective users of information and ideas" (1). This is followed by seven specific objectives and five key challenges related to meeting those objectives. Local schools and districts will need to adapt these guidelines to their own local conditions.

According to Gittell and Flynn (1995), the recent experience of Wang Laboratories illustrates the importance of attention to mission. Wang might have avoided bankruptcy had its core mission been better influenced by such re-examination. This could have encouraged less reliance on a declining market for proprietary minicomputer systems and directed Wang toward product development more in keeping with emerging markets. Having learned its lesson well, Wang has redrawn its core mission in the light of emerging conditions, and is now reappearing as a vital developer of imaging software and workgroup networking (Crosariol 1995).

Some planners feel that senior managers should not unduly influence the development of the core mission statement. They feel that the organization's human creativity is best tapped without such guidance, because "guidance" encourages staff to respond more to their perception of what management wants to hear than to their own best instincts. In practice, planners might do best by responding to their unique organizational cultures. If an organization's history is marked by effective, participatory management, then the organizational culture will help hold the process together and guide it toward successful resolution, whether or not senior managers establish the initial framework for the creation of a mission statement.

On-line examples of school mission statements are available at the Sachem, N.Y., Central School District Web site:

**http://www.sachem.k12.ny.us/blt/**

# Needs Assessment and Environmental Scanning

**ACCURATE NEEDS ASSESSMENT AND REALISTIC SCANNING** of the internal and external program environment are two particularly important planning steps. Without them, planning occurs in an information vacuum, unable to pinpoint constituent needs, program deficiencies, or potential sources of support. In addition to a hard look at current conditions, environmental scanning looks forward and backward. Future school scenarios are envisioned in terms of mission and pedagogy. These take into account anticipated trends in society and the economy. Current inventories of equipment, space, software, materials, and personnel are reviewed with a view to marshaling them more effectively and efficiently. All available resource niches are identified so as to examine all possibilities for mutually advantageous pooling.

When media librarians scan and document their existing school programs, they are performing the "what is" part of a needs assessment. After considering plausible futures and stakeholder interests, they determine "what should be." The difference between the two equals the program need.

$$(\text{What Should Be}) - (\text{What Is}) = \text{Need}$$

## Assessing Needs

There are two basic approaches to needs assessment. One is to limit the assessment only to key persons within the program's service population; the other is to survey the community as a whole (including students and parents). The advantage of the first approach is that the key persons (e.g., school administrators, department heads) are deeply familiar with the relationship between the library media program and the surrounding school environment. Moreover, such a limited assessment lends itself to straightforward methods for collecting data, often through personal interviews or simple written surveys.

Such a narrowly focused assessment strategy carries risks, however. By themselves, key personnel may represent a singular vested interest, keen to maintain the status quo and isolated from valuable opinions present in a broader population of potential stakeholders. Assessing the needs of broader populations can strengthen the base of library media support, especially when assessment results lead to challenging program improvements.

Needs may be assessed in a variety of ways: written surveys, interviews, suggestion boxes, personal observations, and structured information gathering (for example, at academic department or PTA meetings). Locally networked computer bulletin boards are especially useful instruments for assessing needs. Written instruments should be short. Questions should address essential issues only, preferably on one-page instruments pilot-tested among trusted colleagues before general distribution. By the same token, personal interviews and public information-gathering sessions should be objective, uniform, and carefully administered so that the critical information is not lost in aimless, marginally relevant discussion.

Once gathered, the needs assessment data hold much potential for strengthening constituent support for the library media program. Such information affords the opportunity to publicize strengths and to articulate plans for addressing unmet needs.

## Beyond Needs: Scanning Environments

A regular scan of the external and internal environments that daily affect program operations can help media librarians avoid crisis management. It allows them to look closely at the conditions that will influence the shape and direction of a timely plan. Program scanning can begin with a review of the needs assessment results and evaluation of the most recent operational plan: What were the goals? Were they achieved? Why were some achieved and others not? What changes have occurred in the past year that require re-examination of programs for the year ahead? Do the goals contribute to the achievement of the program's core mission? An environment scan will reveal opportunities and pitfalls. Effective scanning helps managers prevent crises by seizing anticipated opportunities and adjusting proactively to known pitfalls.

Here is a simple example. You are a district library media director. At the elementary level, your district is moving toward project based learning and collaborative teaching. Your program's core mission was recently refined. It now reads, "to improve curriculum through the effective, systemwide infusion of electronic media." Two subsidiary program goals are:

- to make curriculum-specific visual materials available to classrooms easily and conveniently
- promote cross-disciplinary teaching and learning through shared access to electronic resources

In past years, this core goal was met by the circulation of video programs, slides, posters, and illustrated books. Recently, however, the district connected every elementary school classroom to the districtwide LAN with two networked multimedia computers per classroom. Additionally, there is a ten-computer lab in each library media center, also connected to the LAN.

Last year, the district gained Internet access through a nearby state college. The prospect of the district soon becoming its own Internet node is being considered. Under pressure from the community, budgets for more traditional library media resources have been severely cut to help pay for the district's computer network development. Somehow, the shortfalls left by the decline in funds for traditional materials will have to be made up from other sources.

After consulting with your district administration, your curriculum department heads, and your staff, you believe that your idea to phase out your district's earlier reliance on expensive stand-alone software and locally networked integrated learning systems will enhance your capacity to serve your district. Scouring the Internet on behalf of your teaching colleagues, you may now find curriculum-specific materials and interactive projects more efficiently and less expensively than ever before. Such a change, however, may disturb a few recalcitrant teachers and will certainly require a redeployment of staff duties. Because of the spadework you have done with your colleagues and your staff, you are confident of sufficient internal support as the service changes unfold.

Two additional McKenzie (1994b; 1994c) documents may help with the assessment of needs and current program conditions:

**http://www.pacificrim.net/~mckenzie/techsurvey.html**

**http://www.pacificrim.net/~mckenzie/questions.html**

Additional insight comes from the results of a technology-oriented library needs assessment conducted at the University of Tennessee, Knoxville (LeClercq 1995). This report resides at:

**http://www.lib.utk.edu/utkpubs/infoissues/NeedsAssess.html**

## Outputs and Goals

**THE FEDERAL GOVERNMENT PERFORMANCE AND RESULTS ACT** of 1993 (GPRA) defines *output* as "the tabulation, calculation, or recording of activity or effort. An outcome measure, as defined by GPRA, is an assessment of the results of a program activity compared to its intended purpose" (Scozzens 1995). Section III of Susan Scozzens's on-Web discussion of organizational performance goals provides an additional perspective. Her report was written for the National Science Foundation in response to GPRA mandates. It may be found at:

**http://www.nsf.gov/od/ops/gprafnl.htm**

Planning outputs are very specific. They describe improved program conditions in quantifiable terms. (An output example is: "Voluntary teacher attendance at staff development events sponsored by the library media center will increase from thirty percent to fifty percent of the elementary school faculty.")

After looking at the outputs described for the current operational plan and examining environmental factors that can promote or hinder fulfillment of the core mission, the process begins to determine how the program should operate in the year ahead. The difference between "what is" and "what should be" describes needs that the new plan is designed to fill. These gaps can generate and justify general goal statements to support the launch of new initiatives.

Let us look at our earlier example of the goal to promote cross-disciplinary teaching and learning through shared access to electronic resources. From one year to the next, this goal may remain unchanged. The program outputs, however, might adjust to the changed environment. Powerful, networked computers are now in sufficient supply to serve an initial phase of anticipated faculty and student needs. Through access to Web and Gopher sites, e-mail, and publicly available computer files, the capacity exists to launch a variety of student projects on the Internet. Thus, a quantifiable program output might be to increase the number of teachers using the Internet in the curriculum by a specific number over the previous year. Another could be that the library media program will generate a 75 percent positive rating on a questionnaire about the Internet support activities of the library media program. The trick, of course, will be to select wisely and in concert with the curricular needs of teachers and children.

## Program Inputs and Responsible Staff

**PROGRAM OUTPUTS DESCRIBE DESIRED FUTURE CONDITIONS.** Inputs describe what must be done to get there. Returning again to our cross-disciplinary teaching and learning example, one of the outputs was to increase teacher use of the Internet. What key inputs are necessary for this output to be realized? Specific Internet resources for staff development (see chapter 4) must be found to support new pedagogies and curriculum integration techniques. Network maintenance will require additional attention. Particular resources will have to be screened, cataloged, and aligned with ongoing curricula. Appropriate staff development must be organized with sufficient publicity to attract participation. A legion of other input tasks could be described in detail, but this is not necessary; only *key* items must be described.

Staff will need appropriate assignments to get new inputs into play. Here again, affected staff should be consulted so that they can voice their concerns, indicating what they need for support so that the media librarian can take proactive measures to deal with anticipated trouble spots. Part of this support will take the form of plan-related staff development. Chapter 4 discusses this subject in detail. Other helpful sources can be found on the Internet. An excellent example comes from Futoran and Wertheimer (1995) in a Web monograph entitled *Professional Development and the Internet: Experiences of Common Knowledge* (written for Common Knowledge, a Pittsburgh-based consortium of schools, higher education, and private business). This document is available at:

http://info.ckp.edu/publications/publications.html

# Budget, Implementation, and Evaluation

**AT THE END OF THE PLANNING PROCESS** comes the budget. A good plan then becomes a powerful tool for budget requests. Once the new budget is negotiated, planners need to make the necessary adjustments. Some goals may have to be dropped, or, if maintained, program outputs may have to be scaled back. Other goals may be added. The point is that although planning and budgeting are dynamically connected, planning comes first!

Although the operational plan describes activity for specified time periods, implementation is a continuing process, subject to review, reassessment, and evaluation at any time. A good plan contains its own summative and formative evaluation processes. A *summative evaluation* is a final accounting of relative success in achieving the goals of a plan. It is keyed to specific criteria defined in the plan's stated outputs and is reported to program stakeholders at the end of a specified period.

*Formative evaluations* of progress are designed for offering feedback, especially during the early stages of plan implementation. They are less formal and more private than summative evaluations and serve as evaluative milestones between the beginning and end of an operational planning period. They produce output progress reports and recommend remedial action when interim outputs prove difficult to produce. Summative results are shared with program staff and reported to superiors and constituents. In contrast, formative evaluations are usually discussed only with program staff.

After the planning process is aligned to the realities of the new program budget, the library media program has a blueprint for upcoming activity. (Figure 2.3 shows a format for the operational plan document. The format can be in table, narrative, or some other form, but whatever form is selected should be concise and readily grasped by all stakeholders.) Implementation is the hardest part, but is much easier with a commonly owned, well-documented plan. Because all planning is part prophecy, and because no one can predict the future with certainty, the plan and its implementation should allow for unforeseen contingencies.

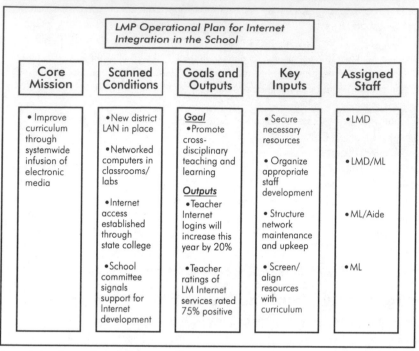

**Figure 2.3   Operational plan template**

For an additional outlook on program budgeting, the following Web file from the cash-strapped Austin Independent School District may be helpful:

**http://www.austin.isd.tenet.edu/budget_rpt.html**

This resource might be supplemented by the document, *What Is a Program Evaluation?* from the Program Evaluation Division of the Minnesota Office of the Legislative Auditor (MOLA 1995):

**http://www.auditor.leg.state.mn.us/wha-pe.htm**

# Rich Resources for Technology Planning

**THE INTERNET IS A VERY POWERFUL INFORMATION SOURCE** for effective educational planning. A good way to start is to check out the initiatives of sister schools. The Web 66 Web server at the University of Minnesota offers an interactive directory of planning resources and "hot-linked" school sites through its International WWW Schools Registry at:

**http://web66.coled.umn.edu/schools.html**

Of the countless resources on the Web, the U.S. Department of Education is not only rich in its own right, but also provides kindred links to other excellent locations. This site is found at:

**http://inet.ed.gov/Technology/**

Headquartered at Mississippi State University, the National Center for Technology Planning (NCTP) is a first-rate clearinghouse for educational technology planning information. In addition to housing exemplary plans, this service offers a variety of Internet-accessible resources germane to planning. NCTP can be reached on the Web at:

**http://www2.msstate.edu/~lsa1/nctp/index.html**

or (a less comprehensive menu) at:

**Gopher://msstate.edu:70/11/Online_services/nctp/**

The NCTP site includes very rich links to other national, state, and local locations. Of particular interest is the "under construction" work of Anderson (1996) and his graduate students, the *Guidebook for Developing an Effective Instructional Technology Plan*, and the more recent companion audio commentary. (The audio files are presented in the RealAudio format and need a 28.8 kbps—or faster—connection to be heard properly. See chapter 1 for additional reference and the Web site for downloading the RealAudio software.)

Earlier, we mentioned the school technology planning guide produced by the Massachusetts Software Council, *The Switched-On Classroom.* Many other relevant resources reside on the Internet. Some of these are particularly germane to media librarians; others are more generic. The Ohio Department of Education (1994) has developed a helpful HyperCard-based technology planning template (see its home Web site in the following list). Following well-accepted planning principles, this tool encourages planners to carry out a process according to five elements:

- establishing a planning group
- developing mission and vision statements
- setting goals
- creating action plans
- evaluating plans and results

Internet search engines and meta search engines (see chapters 6 and 7) will produce valuable hits. As indicated at the start of this chapter, queries to appropriate listservs and newsgroups may also generate many helpful responses. In addition to the resources already mentioned, the following sites will be helpful:

*British Columbia District Technology Planning* (a wide-ranging resource centered on BC's provincial school technology planning initiative. Includes links to more than fifty local district plans)
   British Columbia Ministry of Education
   **http://www.etc.bc.ca/provdocs/disttech/home.html**

*CoSN Technology Planning Electronic Guide* (a hypertext formatted "meta guide" prepared for educators to scan the planning initiatives of other schools and related educational organizations)
   The Consortium for School Networking
   **http://cosn.org/techguide.html**

Diverse resources for school network planning (a well-organized and nicely formatted series of planning aids centered on curricular, technical, and general topics)
>   Champlain Valley Union High School (Vermont)
>   **http://www.cvu.cssd.k12.vt.us/K12TECH/K12TECH.HTM**

*The K-12 Network Technology Planning Guide* (an eleven-chapter, comprehensive planning guide for the state of California, with case studies)
>   California Department of Education
>   **http://goldmine.cde.ca.gov/WWW/Technology/K-12/NTPG/NTPG.html**

*More diverse resources for school network planning* (an exceptionally diverse array of files and documents related to school technology planning)
>   New York State Education Department
>   **Gopher://unix5.nysed.gov/K-12 Resources/Education Technology**

*NASA Ames K-12 Internet Initiative* (a "resource of planning resources" with sharply focused pointers to other planning sites)
>   National Aeronautics and Space Administration
>   **http://quest.arc.nasa.gov/net-learning.html#plan**

*Planning for School Improvement Using Technology* (a five-step planning guide, available as a series of linked HTML files, or by anonymous FTP as a HyperCard document)
>   Ohio Department of Education
>   **http://www.nwoca.ohio.gov/**

*Smart Schools Technical Guidelines* (contains information and resources related to California's Smart Schools partnership. Includes the 142-page book, *Technical Guidebook for Schools*, which requires the Adobe Acrobat Reader software to display and print)
>   Smart Valley, Inc.
>   **http://www.svi.org/PROJECTS/SCHOOLS/index.html**

State-approved school district plans (a growing collection of approved school district technology plans in Massachusetts)
>   Massachusetts Department of Education
>   **http://info.doe.mass.edu/welcome/computer.html**

*Technology Planning and Educational Technology* (Rudy Garns's directory of other Web sites with resources on educational technology and technology planning)
>   University of Northern Kentucky
>   **http://www.nku.edu/~garns/techplan.html**

# A Final Word

**THE LONG-TERM HEALTH** of a library media program will never be secured through day-at-a-time administration. A plan is needed. The plan should be continually updated to reflect changes in the operating environment. It should conform to a compelling vision of service. If this vision is shared by the providers and the consumers of the program's service, successful implementation of the plan is well assured. Planning does not guarantee a sound organization, but without it, organizational health will surely elude even the best intentions.

Like a good short story, effective organizational plans should be spare, simple, and clear. They should be systematic and consistent. Concise planning generates a discipline that promotes logical organization and effective execution. The seventeenth-century French prelate and philosopher, François Fénelon, may not appear in the planning literature, but he advised, "The more you say, the less people remember."

## Notes

1. The following individuals graciously helped identify many of the resources cited in this chapter: George Casler of the New York State Education Department; Melanie Goldman from Bolt Beranek and Newman; Dan Holden of the Northern Buckeye Education Council; Craig Lyndes from the Champlain Valley Union High School; George Perkins of the University of Kentucky; Harry Saal, President of Smart Valley, Inc.; Carole Teach of the California Department of Education; and Karen Traicoff from NASA. Carolyn A. Markuson contributed much of the section on needs assessment.

## References

American Association of School Librarians and Association for Educational Communications and Technology. 1988. *Information power: Guidelines for school library media programs*. Chicago: American Library Association/Washington, D.C.: Association for Educational Communications and Technology.

Anderson, L. 1996. *Guidebook for developing an effective instructional technology plan* [on-line]
Available WWW: **http://www2.msstate.edu/**
Path: **~lsa1/nctp/**
File: **techplan.html**

Becker, H. J. 1994. "How exemplary computer-using teachers differ from other teachers: Implications for realizing the potential of computers in schools." *Journal of Research on Computing in Education* 26(3): 291–321.

Chandler, M. 1994. *The planning commission at work: Enhancing your commission's productivity* [on-line].
Available WWW: **http://www.webcom.com/**
Path: **%7Epcj/articles/**
File: **work14.html**

Cohen, E. 1994. "The architectural and interior design planning process." *Library Trends* 42(3): 547–63.

Crosariol, B. 1995. "Wang Agrees to Pay $20m for Sigma." *Boston Globe*, 18 July.

Deal, T. E., and A. A. Kennedy. 1982. *Corporate cultures: The rites and rituals of corporate life*. Reading, Mass.: Addison-Wesley.

Dede, C. 1993. "Leadership without followers." *Computing Teacher* 20(6): 9–11.

Eisenberg, M. B., and M. K. Brown. 1992. "Current themes regarding library and information skills instruction: Research supporting and research lacking." *School Library Media Quarterly* 20(2): 103–10.

Futoran, G. C., and R. Wertheimer. 1995. *Professional development and the Internet: Experiences of common knowledge* [on-line].
   Available WWW: **http://info.ckp.edu/**
   Path: **Publications/**
   File: **publications.html**

Gittell, R. J., and P. M. Flynn. 1995. "The Lowell high-tech success story: What went wrong?" *New England Economic Review* (March/April): 57–70.

Hockersmith, E. 1994. *Technology planning for libraries* [on-line].
   Available Gopher: **Gopher://ericir.syr.edu:70/**
   Path: **11/InfoGuides/Alphabetical_List_of_InfoGuides/**
   File: **Technology_Plans_for_Libraries-11.94**

Jensen, D. R. 1982. "Unifying planning and management in public organizations." *Public Administration Review* 42(2): 157–62.

LeClercq, A. 1995. *Some good news and some not so good news: The libraries' needs assessment* [on-line].
   Available WWW: **http://www.lib.utk.edu/**
   Path: **utkpubs/infoissues/**
   File: **NeedsAssess.html**

Lorange, P., and R. F. Vancil. 1977. *Strategic planning systems.* Englewood Cliffs, N.J.: Prentice-Hall.

MacDonald, R. M. 1995. "Using Internet resources to enhance school media center services." *School Library Media Quarterly* 23(4): 265–69.

Massachusetts Software Council. 1994. *The Switched-On Classroom: A Technology Planning Guide for Massachusetts Classrooms.* Boston: Massachusetts Software Council.

Mastraccio, M. 1995. *Technology planning for schools* [on-line].
   Available Gopher: **Gopher://ericir.syr.edu:70/**
   Path: **11/InfoGuides/Alphabetical_List_of_InfoGuides/**
   File: **Tech_Plans_Schools-12.95**

McKenzie, J. 1993. *Staff development for new technologies* [on-line].
   Available WWW: **http://www.pacificrim.net/**
   Path: **~mckenzie/**
   File: **staffd.html**

McKenzie, J. 1994a. *Key planning concepts* [on-line].
   Available WWW: **http://www.pacificrim.net/**
   Path: **~mckenzie/**
   File: **criteria.html**

McKenzie, J. 1994b. *Technology planning questions* [on-line].
   Available WWW: **http://www.pacificrim.net/**
   Path: **~mckenzie/**
   File: **questions.html**

McKenzie, J. 1994c. *Technology self-assessment form* [on-line].
   Available WWW: **http://www.pacificrim.net/**
   Path: **~mckenzie/**
   File: **techsurvey.html**

Minnesota Office of the Legislative Auditor. 1995. *What Is a Program Evaluation?* [on-line].
   Available WWW: **http://www.auditor.leg.state.mn.us/**
   File: **wha-pe.htm**

Ocasio, L., F. Gray, and A. Palazzo. 1995. "Great technology plans." *Electronic Learning* 14(7): 31–39.

Ohio Department of Education. 1994. *Planning for school improvement using technology* [on-line].
Available WWW: **http://www.nwoca.ohio.gov/**
Path: **information/EdTechnology/**
File: **Technology Planning**

Pratt, D. 1994. *Curriculum planning: A handbook for professionals.* Fort Worth, Tex.: Harcourt Brace College Publishers.

Scozzens, S. 1995. *Performance assessment at the National Science Foundation* [on-line].
Available WWW: **http://www.nsf.gov/**
Path: **od/ops/**
File: **gprafnl.htm**

# Chapter 3

# School Library—Community Links with the Internet

> Only a strong, unified public spirit will generate the deeds necessary
> to elevate our schools to the level that our children deserve.
>
> *Bruce Joyce (1986)*

## Background in School—Community Internet Links

**MUCH HAS BEEN WRITTEN** about school—community relations and parental involvement. Schools have viewed community involvement as both a positive factor and a negative factor over the past decades. In the 1930s, schools were closed institutions, and learning took place apart from the social setting. In the 1950s, teachers were autonomous and the principal acted as a buffer between parents and the classroom. In the 1980s and 1990s, James Coleman, Robert Crowson, and others proposed that schools should be "community creating" institutions (Crowson 1992). Schools are encouraged to contribute to the "social capital" of the community (Coleman and Hoffer 1987) by adding value to the social networks and the interaction between adults and children in the community.

This book takes the view that linkages between the school and the family or the community at large are to be encouraged when they contribute to student learning and to the lifelong learning of the community. Closer involvement with the community is stressed, with possible areas of involvement being parental involvement in school activities, community participation in strategic planning, parental representation on school improvement councils, and joint school–community committees to plan changes in the school. As Peter Senge points out, in the self-renewing school, that is, "schools where ... really significant innovations ... have endured, they've usually grown out of people from ... multiple constituencies working ... in concert with people in the community who are very much part of the innovation" (O'Neil 1995, 21).

School libraries have been pursuing community linkages of their own over the past few decades, ranging from sharing reading lists with the town library to jointly automating their collections as part of a regional library network. This chapter opens with an overview of more traditional school library–community linkages and then examines ways in which the Internet expands those opportunities. The last half of the chapter looks in detail at four examples of school library–community links that have been shaped by Internet opportunities.

## Promoting the School Library Media Program in the Mind of the Community

Public relations is an important consideration in preserving and promoting the library media program. It is no surprise that library media programs are subject to budget cuts. Promotion of the services of the library media center is important to survival. In this age of expensive new electronic resources, the library budget cannot remain as it has been, and certainly cannot be cut, if we are to provide exposure to on-line and CD-ROM resources and experience with the resources of Internet. Syracuse University's Donald Ely (1981) points up the need to educate the community concerning the valuable role of the library media center in the education of schoolchildren and the central role libraries play in the curriculum. Ely specifies a number of channels for communicating the importance of the library media program to the community and to other practitioners. Depending on the audience and the message, such channels as newsletters, bulletin boards, meetings, mass media, and combinations of these may be appropriate to educate the public.

The Internet can assist with public relations in many ways, from informal e-mail announcements to a well-designed library home page. Keefe, Taylor, and Karpisek (1986) suggest a four-phase approach to successful public relations: research, planning, action, and evaluation. Research involves finding the groups in the community that should be influenced and understanding how they currently perceive the library media program. Planning includes setting goals and objectives, generating and weighing options, and building a base of support. As chapter 2 pointed out, this base of support may include principals, central office personnel, town officers, influential parents, and other key persons in the community. Only after this groundwork has been laid is the media librarian ready to take action through training sessions, newsletters, presentations, or whatever means have been deemed likely to be effective. This phase may require repetition and follow-through. Constant feedback and evaluation are key to success.

Public relations does not simply mean influencing the community. Ongoing communication within the school and with parents is important to the visibility of the library media program. In many schools, the library media center is the hub of the school, sometimes by virtue of its physical location, but more often because an active media librarian takes the lead in disseminating information—about upcoming programs, Internet resources, new books and media, courses and workshops being offered in the area, grant opportunities, and conferences being held. The active media librarian also disseminates success stories to the administration to be used as appropriate in promoting the successful work of the school as a learning organization. Most students use the library media center, and the media librarian is privy to information about many curricular activities, especially projects. In this regard, the media librarian is in a unique position to see across disciplines and grade levels, to reinforce good teaching and learning, and to promote collaboration among faculty.

Communication with parents may not be as easy for the media librarian as for the classroom teacher. The librarian cannot normally send a note home with a student or call a parent conference. However, parent volunteers are effective conduits of information and ideas back to the community. Effective programs, current resources shortages, and potential learning opportunities are more apparent to the parent volunteer who works in the media center a few hours a week, and the media librarian can encourage volunteers to spread the word proactively.

Other traditional means of promoting the visibility and importance of the library media program involve inviting members of the community to speak to students in the library or inviting secondary-level students to read stories they have written to younger students and then videotape or broadcast the sessions over local cable channels (Keefe, Taylor and Karpisek 1986).

## School–Town Library Links

Cooperation with the public library is another traditional way of linking the school library with the community. The public library is often open later in the day than the school library, and on weekends, and it is natural for the public library to support student projects and research. Communication between the school librarian and the town librarian through such means as booklists, notices of upcoming projects, or involvement in the annual science fair can ensure that resources are available for students. Schools should consider encouraging the town librarian to participate in occasional faculty meetings that deal with curriculum changes, with the aim of sharing knowledge of local resources and setting up cooperation between libraries in support of the new curriculum. Another avenue for collaboration is an inservice program run jointly by the public librarian and the school librarian.

The America 2000 Library Partnership (Office of Educational Research and Improvement [OERI] 1992) actively promotes and publicizes greater collaboration between public and school libraries and innovative uses of library resources that benefit all learners in the school and in the community. America 2000 views the country as "a nation of learners" and emphasizes services for lifelong learning. Much like Crowson's view of schools as "community creating" institutions, this is a view of the community as actively engaged in learning in collaboration with the school system. This theme is repeated throughout the examples in this chapter. This view of school and community as partners in education is supported and enhanced by Internet linkages. An online description is available at

**http://www.ed.gov/pubs/parents/Library/Partnership.html**

# Internet Extensions to Traditional School–Library Community Linkages

HOW CAN INTERNET ACCESS enhance and promote school library services for lifelong learning in cooperation with the community? Some applications are obvious. For example, the use of electronic mail can speed communication between the school and town libraries or between the school and parents. With access to e-mail, librarians do not need to schedule meetings or travel between buildings to exchange lists of resources or schedules of curriculum projects with the town library. The libraries can also include each other on distribution lists announcing special events or changes in hours or services.

The media librarian can use two ERIC InfoGuides as good starting points for involving public librarians in an exploration of Internet resources. Beth Vella's *Internet Resources for Public Librarians* (Vella 1994) and Lawrence Carey's *Internet Use for Public Librarians* (Carey 1994) are available at:

### Gopher://ericir.syr.edu:70/11/InfoGuides/

If one of the institutions—town or school library—supports a Web home page or a Gopher server, it can post information on behalf of the others, and it can provide links to rich sources of information likely to be used by librarians or patrons, including parents, at any of the libraries in town. Such a service could also extend to others in the community.

The vast resources of the Internet extend the collections of libraries, opening global resources to the school and community. As noted in chapter 4, the media librarian is uniquely qualified to introduce users to this vast storehouse and to help them develop skills and habits for productive use. Workshops, newsletters, information bulletins, and awareness presentations are excellent vehicles for educating the community about the Internet and, coincidentally, about the school library media program.

On the downside, the Internet poses a problem that is best handled in cooperation with parents—that is, the availability of inappropriate material on the Internet. The media librarian would do well to involve parents and the town librarian, along with school administrators and teachers, in developing an acceptable use policy for students on the Internet and for brainstorming ways to provide adequate network supervision for students. Librarians will be expected to take a lead role in this matter, because they have been dealing with the issue of censorship for many years (see chapter 5 for further discussion).

# Involvement with a Pivotal Community Group: The School Technology Planning Committee

THE PRECEDING ARE A FEW SIMPLE EXAMPLES of school–community links involving the Internet. In actual practice, funding to support widespread Internet use in the curriculum and in the school library media program is usually significant enough to be scrutinized by those in the community who are concerned with the school budget. Schools and communities often collaborate on technology planning for the schools through the formation of a technology planning committee.

Typically, technology planning committees are comprised of school administrators, teachers, parents, and others in the community. The technology planning committee is an example of a community group that has to be educated concerning the library media program and the effective use of the Internet in the schools. Properly educated, the committee members are in a pivotal position to "sell" the rest of the community on the use of the Internet and the preferred mode of access to the rich resources that the Internet provides for student learning. Discussions about Internet use arise in concert with discussions about funding for new computers, funding for a technology coordinator, funding for technology staff development, and networking in the schools.

Some in the community, especially those who work in business and industry, are likely to be very knowledgeable about technology infrastructure (hardware, software, and networks), its costs, and the demands it makes on maintenance budgets and staffing. However, they are less likely to understand the impact on the learning environment and the potential impact on the curriculum. It is not unusual for a community member to think of technology's benefit in terms of increased SAT scores, rather than in terms of increased opportunities for collaborative problem solving and for communication with students around the world on matters of the environment and global relations. The media librarian will want to demonstrate to the community that new learning environments call for new approaches to evaluation.

The technology planning committee can easily lose sight of student learning and achievement when matters of cost and connectivity (or networking) arise. The media librarian and other school personnel on the committee should be prepared to champion the cause of student achievement and to speak for the Internet's benefits to the curriculum. This person should also be prepared to speak realistically about the difficulties inherent in Internet use and staff development for use of the Internet and other telecommunication services.

School technology committees tend to undervalue the strengths of librarians, just as communities have undervalued the role of the library media program in the curriculum of the school. The media librarian would do well to promote the library media program through expert participation on such committees! After all, the media librarian has unique qualifications to explore, acquire, and manage information resources, such as those on the Internet. The media librarian can organize and manage the task of tracking software licenses and can develop policies and procedures related to acceptable use of electronic information resources and circulation of expensive media. All of these strengths are invaluable in protecting and maximizing the community's investment in costly technology.

We have looked at several ways that the Internet can expand and enhance traditional links between school and community, particularly between the school library and the learning community. The media librarian brings a valuable perspective and unique skills to the matter of technology management and planning in support of curriculum. The media librarian's contribution is important not only to the learning community, but also to the promotion and support of the library media program, which is at the center of learning activities in the school.

The remainder of this chapter gives four examples of school–community collaborations that involve the Internet. Each illustrates a different aspect of school library–community involvement with the Internet.

# Examples of School Library–Community Links with the Internet

**ACROSS THE COUNTRY,** school library–community links are appearing and changing as a result of the Internet. The following examples illustrate the variety of roles the media librarian can play in linking school and community through Internet use. Each of the four examples is based on actual school–community linkages, although some are composite examples of several similar cases, and some details have been changed to highlight a particular aspect of school–community partnerships. Sources for the examples are various listservs, annals of technology planning studies, and informal discussions with librarians and technology coordinators in many towns and school districts.

The first example is a major effort in a small city to renovate its inner-city elementary school, expanding the library and the adult education program, and providing Internet access to school and community. The second deals with one town's effort to automate its library holdings and to provide network access to the collection and Internet resources. A third example illustrates the imperative of cooperation with the community's goals to win new services for the library. A final example shows a new trend in town networking that relieves much of the technology support burden from the school and allows the school to focus on curriculum enrichment through networking.

## Example 1: Enhancement of an Inner-City Adult Education Program Through a New Learning Resources Center

A dilapidated inner-city elementary school in a small mid-Atlantic city was receiving Chapter One funding for its large population (90 percent) of underserved children. It applied for and received a federal grant for renovation, with a significant portion of the funding earmarked for adult education. The renovation plans included expansion of the library media center and the addition of a large computer lab adjacent to it. The lab was to be used during the school day for students. After school and evenings, the lab would serve the adult education program, with emphasis on skills development and retraining for the large population of unemployed in the city.

The media librarian participated in the planning effort for the new Learning Resources Center, as it was called. Initial plans called for automation of the library with a link to the regional library network. The new lab, which was to be adjacent to the library, was to hold sixty computers, with an integrated learning system (ILS) on a local area network (LAN). A shared network modem would provide access to telecommunication services from the library and the lab.

The architect for the project, alert to changes in technology, recommended that the school look into additional networking, and the architectural firm hired a team of educational consultants to work with the school in planning the network. The media librarian and the computer coordinator for the school had some Internet exposure and were eager to involve others in use of the Internet. They offered to be involved in the effort to design the network and to plan network services.

At the same time, teachers were unhappy with the recommendation that the school purchase only an ILS, a "glorified workbook" in their view. They wanted additional software and electronic reference tools to support a variety of educational functions. They formed a committee to investigate exemplary software for the elementary curriculum and asked the librarian to advise them regarding CD-ROM reference tools.

## Outreach to the Community

The scope of services to be provided to the community by the new Learning Resources Center was much broader than a traditional school library media center. Because the library media center was at the heart of the new Learning Resources Center, the media librarian was involved in many aspects of planning and managing the center. The media librarian's expertise with information resources and information services was important to the success of the new center.

The adult population to be served by the expanded adult education program included a large Hispanic and Asian population, many with no English language skills and with little training for work in area business or industry. They needed instruction in English, reading and writing, basic math, cultural and social interaction, and such survival skills as filling out forms and applying for assistance and for jobs. The library media center at the school was not accustomed to providing any of these services, and yet the new computer lab was expected to support all of them. The media librarian worked with representatives from the community and the adult education program to set expectations and phase in services.

Staff had to consider the unfamiliar idea of sharing facilities with community members. Initially, they decided that the computer lab would be restricted to use by students and teachers during the school day and then opened to scheduled adult education classes during the afternoon, evening, and weekend hours. During those after-hour periods, an instructor would take responsibility for the security of the library and the lab. Eventually, the lab could be open for general use on an as-needed basis, but such usage would require a lab assistant to be available to support adult use of software and other network resources. The community saw this as an opportunity for adults to train as lab assistants and to learn how to manage computer and network resources. A committee was formed to carry out this idea.

The media librarian recommended that the Learning Resources Center provide a number of information services for the community, with help from volunteers and students. First, a group of adults could train in use of the Internet and then monitor various listservs and newsgroups for information on parenting, public assistance, consumer affairs, the job market, and so on. Newsletters could be prepared quickly using the electronic information and the desktop publishing capability of the new lab. This service would be useful to the community, would give adults an opportunity to exercise their word processing and desktop publishing skills, and would provide good public relations for the school. Students or community volunteers could be asked to translate key information for publication or for announcement on local radio stations.

A new course was planned to train high school students in the city to assist in the lab as tutors, in preparing resumes, in filling out forms, and in providing technical support to adults. The students would receive high school credit for the course, and the work would appear on their resumes or their applications for college or jobs. The students would also take responsibility for compiling an on-line library of standard forms (for tax purposes, job applications, public assistance applications, and so on) and templates for business letters and resumes. This activity would give them experience with gathering, organizing, and providing information, as well as real-world experience with forms and data.

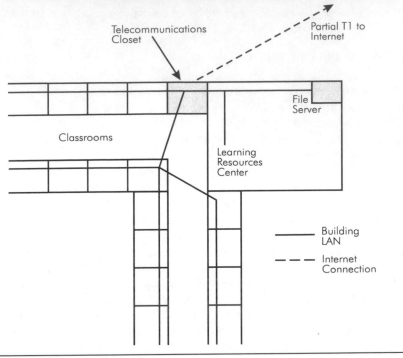

**Figure 3.1    Direct Internet connection**

## Expanded Networking

The consultants and the committee investigating networking in the renovated school had several objectives:

- Make electronic information resources available to classrooms

- Gain access to regional and state library services

- Provide Internet access to as many classrooms and students as possible

- Provide support for portfolios and publication of student work

They designed the building network (see figure 3.1) to support these objectives. Because the school was undergoing extensive renovation, the time was right to extend a data network throughout the building, with drops to each classroom. Although the purchase of multiple computers per classroom was not in the budget for the next few years, it was decided that existing classroom computers would be fitted with Ethernet cards and connected to a building-wide LAN. New computers for the library itself would also be networked.

Access to electronic information resources included the automated library catalog, CD-ROM reference tools, and a variety of databases created by the librarians in support of curriculum. The committee envisioned teachers and students accessing electronic encyclopedias or other on-line references during lessons that called for checking facts or adding to the information available through classroom resources. Teachers and students could also use the network to look at booklists available in the library in support of classroom projects. Teachers could use the network to browse the card catalog from home or from the teachers' lounge and could automatically reserve materials that were particularly relevant to an upcoming activity.

The committee especially wanted teachers and students to be able to access the Internet from the classroom or the lab in support of instructional activities. The media librarian also felt it would give the staff an advantage to have regular access to Internet communications, to participate in newsgroups and listservs and to communicate through e-mail among themselves and with a variety of educators in other locations. A single shared modem would not support these activities.

The committee weighed the relative costs of several dedicated phone lines and modems against the cost of a direct Internet connection for the school. Because the building would be networked, it was more cost-effective to purchase a frame relay connection with 56-kilobit-per-second capacity (one fraction of full T1 capacity) and a LAN bridge between the Internet line and the buildingwide LAN. This would provide direct Internet connection to any computer on the school network, and the high bandwidth would allow simultaneous access from all stations in the lab, classrooms, and the library. As usage increased, the bandwidth could be increased, eventually to full T1 capacity.

The file server planned for the ILS could also serve as an Internet host, receiving news feeds from newsgroups in the Internet and providing electronic mail for the school community. Having a direct Internet connection meant that teachers and students could make use of user-friendly GUI interfaces like Netscape and First Class mail, rather than command line interfaces like Lynx and Pine mail. Those who wanted access from home could dial into the file server using SLIP or PPP connections, and they would also be able to use Netscape and First Class mail from home.

## Exemplary Software Supporting Curriculum

The committee looking into software re-examined the decision to purchase an integrated learning system (ILS) and decided to go ahead with it for several reasons. The new ILS software they investigated had come a long way from the days of the glorified workbook. The package they selected included illustrated literature chosen by a reputable children's publishing house, engaging "story starters" to motivate student writing, journal capabilities with a link to student portfolios, mathematical modeling, spreadsheet tools, and links to third-party software such as word processors and curriculum software. The ILS also included extensive modules for adult learners, especially bilingual, ESL, basic math, and support for GED study. The student population did not have family support for skills practice outside of school, and the ILS would support and track students in this important function. The tracking capability of the ILS also simplified the recordkeeping and communication needed by the many instructors in the community's complex adult education program.

However, the ILS software did not go far enough in support of the cooperative learning activities that teachers wanted to stress with their students. They decided to purchase additional software for their one-computer classrooms that would promote collaborative problem solving and software for the computer lab that would allow them to use it as a writing lab with extensive peer editing and desktop publishing. They added a network license for a hypermedia program, a color scanner, a video camera, and a color printer.

Rather than purchase dozens of CD-ROM titles with the funds available for library titles, the media librarian recommended that they purchase network licenses for a few high-quality CD-ROM titles that were highly relevant to the curriculum, as well as a few specialized titles that could be checked out for individual or classroom use. The media librarian also planned to provide workshops on the use of Internet reference materials and home pages that were especially relevant to the curriculum.

The media librarian saw many uses for the writing and publication tools in the new lab. The lab would have sixty stations, more than enough for two complete classes, so older students could use any free computers for research papers during school hours, making use of the library's electronic reference collection and the software tools in the lab.

The ILS would track the usage of much of the software needed for the new enterprise, but the task of acquiring and inventorying software called for the expert advice of the media librarian. Tracking licenses and upgrades was familiar work for the media librarian, who assisted the Purchasing Department and the computer coordinator in setting up a database to manage them. Policies were drafted concerning circulation of software and electronic reference tools.

## Staff Development Considerations

Providing staff development for the new Learning Resources Center was complicated. *Staff* in this case included teachers, adult education instructors, community/parent volunteers, lab assistants, and others. The media librarian participated on a committee to plan the classes and workshops that dealt with information resources and that recommended classes for staff and community members to learn the ILS, the various writing and publication tools in the lab, and the proper use of expensive peripherals, such as the scanner and video camera.

## Concluding Comments

This example is unusual in the scope of services being developed and implemented relative to a single school. In this case, the community saw a need for improvements in its elementary and adult education efforts and secured funding to support the desired changes. The library was selected as the center of the new facility and was greatly expanded with a new multipurpose computer lab to form a new Learning Resources Center for students and adults in the community. At the same time, advances in networking technology made possible schoolwide access to information services and direct access to Internet resources. This opened opportunities for local and global communications, access to regional and global information resources, and opportunities for curriculum enhancement.

The role of the media librarian in this case was limited only by the individual's knowledge, willingness, and personal energy. The benefits to the learning community—both schoolchildren and adult learners—were many, and the media librarian contributed significantly to these new learning opportunities.

## *Example 2: Shared Cataloging with Public Library*

The preceding example is posited on a large budget and commitment from a large number of community concerns. Not every community is in this situation. However, it is not unusual for a school library–community link to begin with an idea or a need that originates in the community.

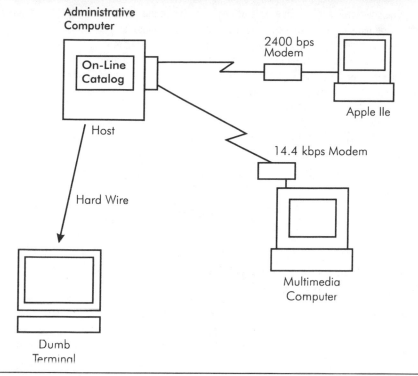

Administrative
Computer

On-Line
Catalog

2400 bps
Modem

Apple IIe

Host

14.4 kbps Modem

Hard Wire

Multimedia
Computer

Dumb
Terminal

**Figure 3.2    Shared catalog**

The media librarian at a school in a small midwestern community was eager to involve students and teachers in the use of the Internet; members of the town wanted to automate the town library and make it part of a regional library network. The town budget could not support automation without taking funds away from the school budget. Because the school also wanted to automate its library holdings, a committee was formed to investigate ways that the town and school libraries could cooperate in providing on-line information access for school and community.

The town was able to support a phased implementation that began with automation of the joint holdings for the town and high school libraries. The on-line catalog database was maintained on the school's business department computer. A seldom-used terminal was moved from the guidance office to the library to provide access for the librarian. An old Apple IIe and an old 2400 bps modem with a long telephone cord were pressed into service for student access to the on-line catalog and to the Internet, using the telephone line in the librarian's office. Access was provided from the town library through a dedicated line, a new multimedia computer, and a 14.4-kbps (kilobits per second) modem donated by a prominent citizen. (See figure 3.2.)

Because there was no statewide telecommunication network for teachers and students, the media librarian applied for an Internet account with a commercial service and shared the account with peers. Internet use in the high school was necessarily limited by the slow-speed access from a single computer. However, the access was adequate for several teachers to monitor listservs and exchange information with others in their departments. Two teachers piloted telecommunication projects using pen pals in other countries and publicized the results of the experience in the local newspaper.

The media librarian offered a workshop for administrators to explore AskERIC and other services for educators available through the Internet. The Assistant Superintendent for Curriculum and Instruction then held a workshop for the committee looking into school reform. As the number of stakeholders grew, so did community support for the new library services and for Internet access. Over the next few years, the school was able to purchase two new multimedia computers with CD-ROM for the library, along with a 14.4-kbps modem and a SLIP or PPP account from a commercial service.

This example illustrates that even meager budgets can support Internet use in some capacity and that effective use by knowledgeable educators can be leveraged to build community support for more resources. This community is unlikely to be able to afford direct connection to the Internet on the same scale as the first or last examples in this chapter, yet the libraries in this town are making good use of networking in support of student learning and the community's information needs.

## Example 3: Library Access to Townwide Network

The library media program can play a large or a small role in community networking. One small, affluent New England town supported a K–8 school system with several elementary schools and a middle school. Graduates of the middle school attended a regional high school or went on to private schools. The community was intent on providing its students with instructional computing experience, with an emphasis on presentation skills and multimedia production. Each school had a computer lab and one or more computers in every classroom. None were connected by networks. The reason given for the lack of networking was the high cost of installing networks in the old school buildings. The administrative computing needs of the district were handled by the computing resources of the town, and the central administrative offices were co-located with the town offices. All communication with the individual school buildings was handled by "SneakerNet"—that is, individuals hand-carried documents and floppy disks from building to building.

To the chagrin of the town librarian, who wanted to automate, the public library was regarded as a traditional repository of print materials, in particular an archive for town historical papers. A similar attitude prevailed with the school libraries. The elementary libraries were regarded as places for storytelling, and library skills meant learning to borrow books and use an encyclopedia. The middle school was chained to the *Reader's Guide* and did not have computers powerful enough to run a multimedia encyclopedia. This town did not want to automate its school or town libraries! The buildings were ivy-covered and the card catalogs were sacred. At town meetings, in response to requests to update the libraries, automation was deemed "crass" and "commercial" and generally at odds with the old values. The media librarian at the middle school and several teachers were intent on promoting the Internet in the schools, but were hampered by the limited access they were able to put together with a personal modem and a small computer borrowed from the lab.

At the same time, the town supported an active population of senior citizens. The senior center adjoined the town and school offices, and a large recreation center for children was at the heart of the complex, complete with swimming pool and skating rink (see figure 3.3).

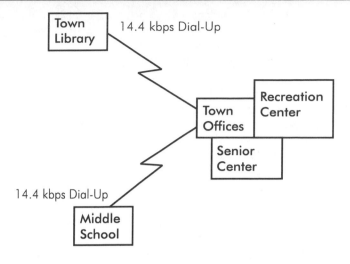

**Figure 3.3    SeniorNet**

The town fathers wanted to increase the involvement of seniors with schoolchildren. Here the media librarian saw an opportunity to further the cause of networking in the schools!

Working as a team, the media librarian, a teacher, and a principal approached the town librarian with a plan to connect seniors and schoolchildren through electronic mail. Dubbed "SeniorNet," the plan involved using the electronic mail capability of the administrative computer, currently used only by central administration and town data processing personnel. Access for participants in the new SeniorNet project would be provided from computers in the libraries. The self-appointed committee approached several seniors and the director of the senior center regarding the project. The seniors were interested, but the idea did not go far enough to suit them. Because they had heard so much about the Internet from the news media, they wanted more than e-mail communication with the students. They wanted to learn to "surf the Net" in earnest! The committee gladly expanded its plan to include instruction in the use of Lynx, which could also be provided through the administrative computer.

The program was piloted in the town library, the middle school library, and the senior center (see figure 3.3). Following the "each one teach one" model (see chapter 4), the media librarian offered a train-the-trainer workshop in use of Internet e-mail and gave participants a feel for the range of information resources available on the Web through Lynx. Seniors used e-mail and Lynx from two new computers at the senior center and one in the town library. Schoolchildren accessed special e-mail accounts created for their classrooms, initially using a computer and modem in the school library. Parents could participate using the connection at the town library. Although parents were not central to this plan, it was felt that parental awareness might further the cause, and their participation gave a stronger reason to connect the town library in the scheme.

By working together, in support of town goals but also with their own agenda, the librarians in this village were able to win town support for Internet access for their libraries. Their

hope was that demonstrating the power of networking and using the public relations channels in place for the SeniorNet project, they would garner support for networking within the
school buildings and classroom access to the Internet.

This example shows the importance of bringing library technology goals into line with
community goals, if possible. The benefits of doing so in this case outweighed the difficulties involved. Although the curricular goals were not fully met in the initial phase, and the
desire for automation was not addressed, an important new linkage between seniors and
students was facilitated, paving the way to meet curricular goals later on.

## Example 4: Townwide Networking

Schoolwide and townwide networking are complex undertakings, as the preceding
examples illustrate. Planning, implementing, and supporting the infrastructure for a high-
speed wide area network (WAN) are difficult and costly tasks. Communities that want to
implement a state-of-the-art network will want to inform themselves about networking
before undertaking the effort. One of two good resources for those undertaking the effort
is the California Department of Education's *Network Technology Planning Guide*, located at:

**http://goldmine.cde.ca.gov/WWW/Technology/K-12/NTPG/NTPG.html**

Another is the Smart Valley, Inc. *Smart Schools Technical Guidebook for Schools
(Networking)*:

**http://www.svi.org/netday/info/guidebook.html**

Occasionally, a community that has been adding to its technology resources for a
number of years, grappling with the issue of keeping its technology infrastructure up-to-
date and running smoothly, decides to create a town/municipal department that will take
responsibility for the town computing infrastructure, including school administrative
computing and instructional computing. A municipality in the Northwest is a case in point.
The town formed a department with responsibility for technology planning throughout the
town, including the school system. The department also managed maintenance contracts
for hardware and software, kept the networks running efficiently, repaired hardware as
needed, contracted for facilities upgrades when new technology was introduced to an old
building, bought hardware and cabling in quantity, ensured compliance with bid laws, and
so on. This arrangement greatly simplified the approach to town networking. The tasks of
negotiating with the cable company, the telephone company, and various contractors were
consolidated.

The town negotiated with its cable television provider to use a few channels from
the cable television institutional loop (I-loop) as the backbone of a townwide data network.
A *backbone* network, like the spinal column of the human nervous system, connects all the
major components or buildings and allows data signals to flow swiftly across a high-
bandwidth wire or, in this case, the cable that also carried cable television signals. The
channels of the I-loop used for data transmission were referred to as the *institutional
network* or *I-net*. Figure 3.4 shows the topology for the I-net in this municipality.

The I-net connected all town buildings—firehouses, hospital, town offices, and so
on—including all of the school buildings. Data flows throughout each building on the
building LAN (if one is in place), reaching any computer connected to the LAN. Adapters,
located in each building where the cable connects to the building, perform the translation
from Ethernet data signals to cable-channel signals and vice versa.

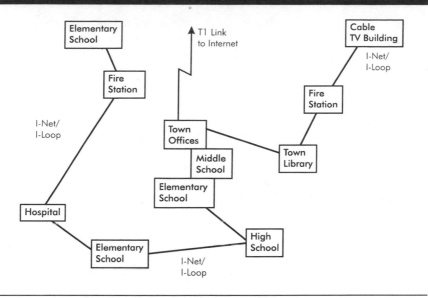

**Figure 3.4    Backbone institutional network (I-Net)**

The town initially investigated a possible connection of the school/town network to the Internet using a direct connection through new frame relay technology, like the connection in this chapter's first example. The town had considered purchasing a bridge that would connect the new network to a T1 line for a direct Internet connection, but decided it could not afford the price with current revenue streams.

However, the investigation sparked interest in the community in providing Internet access to community members for a fee. Various community members had accounts on commercial services and felt that the community would benefit by having its own community Internet service. Just as the community had made extensive use of the cable television capabilities, it could make use of its own Internet capability, if such were available. Community members could provide the services they wanted, create their own home page(s), and have uniform network access to the schools. Parents could communicate with teachers on the progress of students, check on school schedules, call up homework assignments, make suggestions, offer assistance, and so on. As everyone in the town and school would be using the same software interfaces, training and support would be simplified. Parents could join their children with this new dimension of education. (Seniors who had suffered the embarrassment of not understanding New Math enough to assist their children with homework in the late 1950s and early 1960s were vocal about the benefit of this particular point!) Voters expressed an interest and a willingness to support commercial Internet access by and for town residents, and, by extension, the school. The plan moved ahead with the town providing Internet accounts for its citizens and its schools.

## Questions About the Educational Value of the Internet

As with any group's first-time involvement with the Internet, problems arose. Many community members were frustrated in their attempts to find worthwhile resources. Several found their ways to the smut and trash that clutters the Net and, understandably, objected to making these materials available to students. Concerns were voiced about allowing students to have direct access to the Internet—or any access at all! What educational value did the Internet have? How could children be barred or protected from inappropriate material? Only two of the school buildings (the middle and elementary schools adjacent to the town offices) had LANs installed, so citizens put a hold on further installation of school building LANs until the matter was resolved.

The media librarian and several teachers in the middle and elementary schools had already taken the lead in regard to Internet use in the curriculum. Pilot programs were under way incorporating Internet resources in the research process and involving students in pen-pal relationships in support of foreign language and social studies curricula. The educators were able to demonstrate the educational value of the Internet by inviting parents and others in the town to see the projects and discuss the benefits to student learning.

The media librarian took a leadership role in establishing an acceptable use policy for the schools. With the support of her principal and the superintendent, she headed a committee to draft policies and procedures for educational use of the Internet. Their first order of business was an acceptable use policy for students on the Internet. The media librarian drafted one using several examples found on the Internet (see chapter 5) and then guided the committee discussion until a revised policy was adopted.

The media librarian also worked with teachers in other buildings to identify curriculum resources on the Net and possible scenarios to integrate these resources with the K–12 curriculum. These ideas were put before the town as an argument for extending direct Internet access to students at all levels. The town finally moved ahead with its plan to provide LANs for each school building.

## Training for Teachers and Community Members

Training for teachers and for community members was another concern. The media librarian and several knowledgeable teachers were asked to provide classes for the community in Internet use. Initially resistant to providing training for the community, they were offered stipends to organize and launch a program. They adopted a train-the-trainer approach. Those in the community who wanted to become trainers were understandably impressed with the librarian's and teachers' knowledge about the Internet, with their awareness of the issues of student use of the Internet, and with their ability to teach the complex subject. The interaction resulted in new respect on the part of these citizens for school personnel. The word spread, and members of the community gained a new perspective on the school and the school library media program.

## Concluding Remarks

The implementation was not without difficulties, of course, but it allowed the media librarian and others in the school to access the Internet in support of curriculum and to link with the community on important issues. In this community, each obstacle was treated as a challenge and an opportunity. Another example of a problem that confronted this implementation was the need for hotline support, which became apparent as usage increased. The media librarian pointed out that students from the high school were prime candidates for providing telephone and e-mail support. A service was set up employing high school Internet buffs to support the community in exchange for a modest hourly wage and strong letters of reference for their college and job applications.

This example illustrates new services for municipalities and schools that are made possible with networking. Services on a commercial scale are beyond the scope of most schools and require more expertise and support than the media librarian can provide. However, the media librarian can and should play a crucial role in making these community services a reality when they are in line with the learning goals of the school. In this case, the media librarian took a leadership role in regard to integration with the curriculum, acceptable use and other policies, and training for community members. Others in the town and school, such as teachers and students, became involved with curriculum integration and technical support.

## Summary

**THIS CHAPTER GAVE SEVERAL EXAMPLES** to illustrate various kinds of school–community linkages possible with the Internet. In addition to the more obvious connections possible with e-mail and Web home pages, rich opportunities for school–community involvement abound with Internet use and access. These include adult education, on-line access to library resources, participation in planning new school–community technology services, and participation in townwide networking. As with any school–community linkage, the goals of the community and the goals of the school will shape the relationship. When these goals are in conflict, the approach may have to be modified and a base of support built among the key stakeholders.

The media librarian has much to offer the community in its adventures with the Internet. Experience with Internet resources, the ability to organize and manage information resources, expertise with copyright and acceptable use, experience with procedures for tracking and expediting use of critical resources—all these are strengths needed by those who want to venture into the world of the Internet. Such persons will want to draw on the knowledge and teaching skill of the media librarian in undertaking the journey.

## References

California Department of Education. 1994. *Network technology planning guide* [on-line].
Available WWW: **http://goldmine.cde.ca.gov/**
Path: **WWW/Technology/K-12/NTPG/**
File: **NTPG.html**

Carey, L. 1994. *Internet use for public librarians* [on-line].
Available Gopher: **//ericir.syr.edu:70/11/**
Path: **InfoGuides/**

Coleman, J., and T. Hoffer. 1987. *Public and private high schools: The impact of communities.* New York: Basic Books.

Crowson, R. L. 1992. *School–community relations under reform.* Berkeley, CA: McCutchan Publishing.

Ely, D. P. 1981. *Public relations for school media programs.* ERIC Fact Sheet. August; EDRS No. 232 704.

Joyce, B. 1986. *Improving America's schools.* New York: Longman.

Keefe, B., J. Taylor, and M. Karpisek. 1986. "High touch: PR." *School Library Media Quarterly* 14(3): 128–30.

Office of Educational Research and Improvement. 1992. *AMERICA 2000 library partnership.* October; EDRS No. 352 065.

O'Neil, J. 1995. "On schools as learning organizations: A conversation with Peter Senge." *Educational Leadership* 52(7): 20–23.

Smart Valley, Inc. *Smart schools technical guidelines for schools (Networking)* [on-line].
Available WWW: **http://www.svi.org/**
Path: **netday/info/**
File: **guidebook.html**

Vella, B. 1994. *Internet resources for public librarians* [on-line].
Available Gopher: **//ericir.syr.edu:70/11/**
Path: **InfoGuides/**

# Chapter 4 ■

# The Internet, the Library Media Program, and Staff Development

Schools have all too often relied upon the individual teacher's good will and dedication to support training programs.... If teacher pay were on a high professional level, that might be a reasonable expectation, but it is time we showed commitment to training by paying for it.

*Jamie McKenzie (1993)*

*Staff development* can be defined in any number of ways. It may be defined as a series of programs enabling personnel to develop skills and knowledge that will permit schools to attain their objectives (Joyce and Showers 1988). Additionally, staff development offers personal opportunities for professional growth. Ultimately, staff development should be directed toward improved student achievement and learning (Joyce and Showers 1988), as well as overall school improvement (Caldwell 1989).[1]

Before integrating the Internet into subject area curricula, media librarians should think about their role in introducing the Internet throughout the school. The process of integration is connected to the role of leadership exercised by the media librarian and to how that leadership can result in some type of staff development program for teachers and staff members. Before Internet integration can occur in subject areas, teachers must be convinced that using the Internet will offer students improved and expanded learning opportunities. Teachers should also have the chance to learn about the Internet, how it works, what it offers them as professionals, and how it can be infused into specific subject areas.

Internet access to worldwide information brings challenging learning opportunities to the school and the classroom. It is no longer necessary to have all resources available on-site. Instead, using the Internet, off-site databases and other resources may be accessed quickly. The Internet can also be used as a learning tool, with the emphasis on the process of searching for and locating information rather than on the information itself.

# Media Librarian Leadership

**THE INITIAL INTRODUCTION OF THE INTERNET** into the library media program provides opportunities for formal, informal, and inservice staff development. Under firm and careful leadership, the library media program can serve as a staff development center for teachers and staff both in the school and throughout the system. First, however, reflective thought and planning must occur in joint cooperation between the media librarian and other members of the school community (see chapter 2).

*Information Power* (AASL/AECT 1988) defines the three roles of the library media specialist within the school: information specialist, teacher, and instructional consultant. Within the context of staff development, media librarians move across all three roles as they offer technical and instructional support, skill training, services, and information. Deliberate staff development leadership will make the media librarian a key leader in advancing the school's curricular mission. Figure 4.1 shows how the media librarian fulfills these roles in regard to staff development.

As with planning, staff development must be tied to the school and district missions. Staff development should focus on helping the school, its staff, and its students to meet commonly understood goals and expectations (Metzdorf 1989). Otherwise, media and information skills cannot be successfully integrated into the curriculum. The Internet skills training sessions and the staff's subsequent abilities to use the Internet to access information and problem solve are not ends in themselves. Like all tools, the Internet should be merged into present and emerging curricula.

Media librarians are uniquely placed to be their schools' Internet "travel agents." The media librarian should be perceived as an information systems expert in the larger teaching community. As an expert resource, the library media program can identify with the school's technology "pioneers" and also serve as a bridge to the "settlers," providing information, training, encouragement, and support. With *Information Power*'s emphasis on the media librarian's role of instructional consultant, it is natural to organize staff development based on known needs; to serve as an information clearinghouse for school personnel; and to import, organize, and redistribute information from national or global sources.

Teacher skill and expertise will eventually reach a point where attention will shift from introductory skill training to facilitating Internet use for teaching and learning. Media

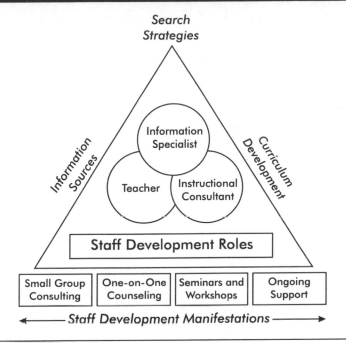

**Figure 4.1   Staff development roles and manifestations**

librarians should be key members of the school's curriculum development team. In this way, they serve as consultants who offer specialized knowledge about research and how resources can be successfully integrated into subject area curricula.

# Useful Strategies for Getting Started

**THE FOLLOWING SECTION** presents information on staff development and:

- logistics and planning
- adoption
- implementation
- continuation
- evaluation

Strategies for the diffusion of faculty skills and knowledge and possible problems and solutions are also outlined. Many staff development models have proven to be highly successful in their proper contexts. Some of these are mentioned in the following pages, and the media librarian can access other staff development information for further review and use (e.g., Loucks-Horsley et al. 1987).

## Theories Behind Staff Development

Change is never easy. It is time-consuming. It also demands effort and money. Change usually involves struggle (Fullan and Stiegelbauer 1991). It is an ongoing process, not a single event (Hall and Loucks 1977; Fullan and Park 1981). Leadership for change is difficult because it requires a constant re-examination of assumptions and beliefs. Success or failure can depend on self-knowledge, knowledge of others, and a willingness to take and tolerate risks, including the risk of failure. Constructive change can thrive in a climate of trust; it founders on pessimism.

Change may result in uncomfortable and stressful situations for those involved in the change process, especially when they are challenged to perform in new and unfamiliar ways. Feelings of ambivalence and uncertainty usually characterize the change process, and these feelings must be worked through and dealt with before the change can be implemented and institutionalized (Fullan and Stiegelbauer 1991).

Adults learn differently than children and young adults, and their learning styles vary. Vandergrift (1994) discusses several useful points about adult learners (specifically teachers) that will help the media librarian to think through the staff development process:

- Participation and motivation are connected to the value that the adults place on the educational experience.

- Respect for the teachers' prior knowledge should be reflected in planning and carrying out staff development.

- Cooperative and peer-group learning will permit the adults to share professional experience and responsibility for their own learning.

- Learning goals must be realistic and the learning pace reasonable.

- The learning experience should challenge learners through a variety of learning resources and activities.

Ellsworth (1994) describes four sequential levels of developmental learning, each deeper level depending on mastery at the preceding level. Ellsworth's framework is summarized in the following:

- Level 1: Why are we doing this? Outcomes are defined. Expectations are set. The Internet's usefulness is established. Connection is made to the larger professional context.

- Level 2: Learning the technology. Participants are given all necessary hands-on exposure to the Internet.

- Level 3: Mastering the tools. Mastery of this level requires learning how to use Internet tools such as WWW and Gopher. To build confidence, time is reserved for practice and play.

- Level 4: Application for problem solving. The participant comes to see the value of the Internet as a means of achieving professional goals.

Media librarians need to consider these principles when they are engaged in staff development. Some teachers have steep learning curves; others may find it difficult to sustain interest in mastering technological procedures that seem difficult or arcane or even irrelevant. Even highly motivated teachers require time to master these skills. A typical group of teachers will not become experts in six or eight weeks; believing otherwise will lead to frustration and discouragement.

## What to Offer and When to Offer It

In its most primitive form, the Internet is not for everyone. Successful users need to have a clear sense of professional purpose to learn how to successfully navigate the Internet's topography. As front-end, user-friendly programs such as Netscape become more readily available, Internet access becomes more transparent. Although that day has not yet come for many schools, this is changing. Until then, the media librarian will need to plan carefully in deciding what to include for whom in staff development for the Internet.

The media librarian must make decisions concerning how to select the first-wave participants in a school. One possibility is to identify the small group of teachers who are eager and willing to learn how to use the Internet. Joyce and Showers (1988) call these eager learners "omnivores." Such people possess the intrinsic motivation to sustain themselves and the confidence to work collaboratively. Omnivores are willing to learn new ways to increase student learning opportunities and are willing to tolerate the risk of failure. These "pioneers" can be recruited at an early phase of Internet training. They serve as successful models for their teaching peers. They also can—and should!—become teachers of teachers.

On the other side of the staff development environment are the reluctant learners, termed "reticents" by Joyce and Showers (1988). In extreme cases, the reticent might flatly refuse to have anything to do with the Internet. Perhaps these reticents should be skipped, and the vast middle ground of teachers ("settlers," as it were) should be targeted for early attention, pulled along with the active help of the omnivores.

## Models for Implementation

Media librarians will have to select the type of staff development program that will be most effective for their schools. Structuring staff development around an accepted model helps ensure success. There are many highly recommended models. The one developed by Joyce and Showers (1988) has withstood the tests of time and experience. It contains five essential elements:

- exploration and discussion of theory
- demonstration or modeling of the necessary skills
- practice of those skills under simulated conditions
- opportunities to receive and give feedback
- peer coaching, under classroom conditions

Peer coaching is the component that facilitates the actual transfer of training, enabling the teacher to consciously and consistently use those new skills and strategies in the classroom to improve student achievement.

McKenzie (1993) builds upon the Joyce and Showers model and offers the following practical framework for staff development in educational technology:

- clarification of expectations
- creation of a staff development planning committee
- design of program offerings (eleven specific guidelines are offered)
- adaptation of the program to specific school needs

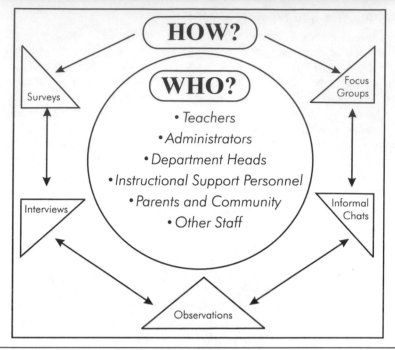

**Figure 4.2    Staff development needs assessment**

## Next Steps

Where does the media librarian go next? As an essential early step, the media librarian should perform a needs assessment to get a feel for the current situation in the school building (chapter 2 discusses needs assessment in greater detail). As shown in figure 4.2, this assessment can use observations, surveys, interviews, and focus group session conversations. It can be formal, informal, or a combination of the two. All the major stakeholders within the school should be surveyed to determine where Internet use can be integrated into subject curricula, how it can be integrated, willingness to participate in Internet staff development, staff learning styles, and staff level of awareness of the Internet and its resources.

Stakeholders may include:

- teachers
- administrators
- department heads
- key instructional support personnel
- other staff members (aides, support staff)
- parents and community members

The needs assessment will help determine the levels of acceptance of and resistance to the Internet. It will provide a framework for structuring the training around staff and subject area needs.

Inservice time for Internet staff development may initially be planned throughout one or two school years, with follow-up support lasting longer. This realistic time frame reflects a typical technology learning curve and allows adequate time for integrating technology into subject curricula.

A variety of times are available for this purpose. These include staff development days, after-school events, teacher planning periods, department meetings, summer sessions, and time "found" through the creative scheduling of classes and teaching assignments. Internet training can dovetail with changes to block scheduling that provide longer time periods for classes and cooperative planning time for teachers and media librarians. Every effort should be made to integrate Internet components with other parts of the staff development program. Technology for its own sake is of little value, but it thrives in the context of the curricular aims of the school.

## What to Teach and How to Teach It

**BECAUSE EACH SITUATION IS UNIQUE,** no single staff development prescription or model applies in all cases. Some objectives for Internet staff development are common to all, such as procedures for login and logout, the use of basic Internet tools, proper netiquette, basic search strategies, identification of Internet resources, ways to access appropriate and usable material, and ways to make use of the Internet part of the curriculum.

Other decisions concerning what to include may differ from building to building. For example, should the arcane FTP process be taught? If so, to whom? One teacher might be excited by the free software that is available through FTP and willing to learn its intricacies, whereas another teacher would rather subscribe to listservs and communicate with colleagues by e-mail. Because many files can be accessed through the Web or by Gopher, only a few teachers may need to master the formal FTP tool. Decisions about appropriate Internet resources will vary, depending on teacher interests, subject matter, and learning needs.

Specific instructional activities (such as on-line demonstrations, worksheets, and small group assignments) can be identified prior to the start of the staff development program. The media librarian would be wise to maintain a large and ongoing file of information sources about the infusion of successful Internet-based projects into a variety of subject curricula. This file can be matched against another database of identified staff needs. This information may include items culled from e-mail and the Internet, articles, and papers. Judi Harris from the University of Texas at Austin has collected and categorized Internet-infused educational activities, a partial collection of which was published in her "Mining the Internet" column in *The Computing Teacher*; the remainder can be accessed from:

**FTP://ftp.tapr.org/pub/ed-telecomputing/telecomputing-info/ed-infusions/**

(see subdirectories by subject). Resource materials of this type should be readily available for staff use both during and after the staff development program.

As Ellsworth (1994) has pointed out, participants should master one level of learning before moving on to the next one. The twelve-session staff development outline shown in figure 4.3 is suggested as a skeleton that conforms to Ellsworth's principles. It can be expanded and fleshed out according to each building's unique situation and needs.

### Internet Basics for Educators: A Staff Development Outline

*Description:*

This staff development unit is an introduction to the "Information Superhighway," which interconnects schools, universities, research centers, corporations, and agencies around the world. Participants will research and develop a pathfinder (a resource guide that lists access routes to information on a specific topic) for their colleagues or students, focusing on Internet resources in a particular curriculum area, and reflecting productive habits for Internet use. This work may be done cooperatively in small groups (see appendix A for an example of a pathfinder).

*Objectives:*

- Master Internet communication tools

- Master Internet research access tools

- Explore, evaluate, and use a variety of Internet resources in an educational context

- Study network configurations that support Internet use in schools

- Discuss the educational issues impacting Internet use in schools

*Topical Outline:*

Session 1.    Overview of the Internet. Expectations for the class. E-mail.

Session 2.    Listservs. Managing information overload. Listserv archives.
              Relevant project models for K-12.

Session 3.    Introduction to Gopher and Veronica.

Session 4.    Introduction of the pathfinder concept as resource guide.
              Pathfinder types.

Session 5.    Introduction to Telnet. Searching ERIC via Telnet.

Session 6.    Introduction to the WWW. Netscape. Implications for curriculum.

Session 7.    Network configurations supporting Internet use. Begin work on
              pathfinder project.

Session 8.    Participant research and project preparation.

Session 9.    Participant consideration of productive search strategies.
              Implications for pathfinder development

Session 10.   Presentation of project plans. Feedback. Policies and procedures
              for Internet access by students.

Session 11.   Participant work on pathfinder.

Session 12.   Presentation of pathfinders. Participant evaluation of sessions.

---

**Figure 4.3    Staff development outline for Internet basics**

# The Internet as a Resource for Staff Development

Honey and Henríquez (1993) found that Internet services are used more for professional purposes than for activities involving student projects and learning. Communicating with colleagues via e-mail was the most widely used staff development activity, followed by accessing and exchanging information on electronic forums and bulletin boards, and locating information in remote databases. Educators seem to view the use of telecommunications as a way to overcome the isolation that characterizes professional life in many schools. This occupational hazard can be partly overcome by the Internet's capacity to enable collegial interaction on a local, national, or global scope.

As the primary information resource for all school personnel, the media librarian becomes a proactive educational leader who plans and orchestrates a teacher-centered staff development program for the Internet. Through its various tools, the Internet provides countless opportunities to access information in remote computers and databases. Because the Internet landscape is always changing, the media librarian can never have a definitive list of all the resources that might be useful for staff development. Translating the riches of the Internet into useful resources for learning, teaching, and training means that media librarians need to find ways to turn the accessed information into a coherent, theory-based staff development program.

## E-mail: Internet Listservs and Electronic Periodicals

As described in chapter 7, simple e-mail provides educators with a way to contact subject- and interest-specific colleagues throughout the world. Such use is easy and relatively inexpensive. Although not a substitute for participation in professional conferences, the results can be similar, in that the colleagues "meet," work with, and learn from each other. Such a situation can be a blessing for media librarians who work alone in schools and need ongoing peer contact to maintain professional vitality. E-mail contact can be initiated on a personal level by swapping e-mail addresses with known colleagues, and by contacts made through conferences or professional organizations. Individual users may form collegial listservs or their own distribution lists for smaller groups of people with whom they work on particular projects.

Listservs of particular interest to the library media staff developer follow. (Refer to chapter 7 for additional resources and guidance for accessing them.)

- CoSN@COSNDISC@list.cren.net (Consortium for School Networking)
- EDTECH@msu.edu (general information about educational technology)
- KIDSPHERE@vms.cis.pitt.edu (K–12 discussion list for people who work with children)
- K12ADMIN@listserv.syr.edu (K–12 administrators, principals, superintendents, and others)
- LM_NET@listserv.syr.edu (school library media community)
- MEDIA-L@bingvmb.cc.binghamton.edu (educational uses of media)
- NETLIBS@qut.edu.au (Australian forum for sharing Internet training ideas with media librarians in K–12 schools; e-mail to: mailserv@qut.edu.au)
- PACS-L@uhupvm1.bitnet.edu (Public Access Catalog Systems Forum)

An electronic newsletter of particular interest to media librarians is ALA-WO (subscription request to

**listproc@ala1.ala.org**).

This newsletter, published irregularly, keeps recipients current with national library and media center issues and legislation. Issues of the *ALA Washington Office Newsline* (ALAWON), available only in electronic form, are e-mailed to each subscriber's mailbox. The ALAWON archives Gopher can be found at:

**Gopher://gopher.ala.org:70/11/alagophwashoff/alagophwashoffnewsline/**

## Remotely Located FTP Files

Many resources available via FTP are particularly helpful for media librarians and other educators. The regularly updated *Internet Resource Directory for Educators* (IRD) is a good place to begin. This is available by anonymous FTP from:

**FTP://ftp.tapr.org/pub/ed-telecomputing/telecomputing-info/IRD**

The IRD has four sections: IRD-ftp-archives.txt, IRD-infusion-ideas.txt, IRD-listservs.txt, and IRD-telnet-sites.txt. The material can be contexted for staff development in several ways: it provides content that can be included in subject area curricula; it supplies teachers with examples of pedagogical ideas and approaches that they can use in their teaching; and it gives examples of effective classroom management strategies. These Internet resources can be used to help improve student achievement and learning and to facilitate overall school improvement.

## Resources by Web or by Gopher

A particularly significant Internet resource, AskERIC, has already been cited several times in this book. A sampling of AskERIC materials includes lesson plans; K–12 Internet projects; state and regional educational information; electronic journals, books, and reference tools; and journal articles, documents, and abstracts. Subjects as diverse as improving the teaching of fractions, learning about information search process models, and outlining and evaluating a two-year program designed to teach high school students on-line searching skills are covered.

AskERIC, available via WWW at

**http://ericir.syr.edu/**

or by Gopher at

**ericir.syr.edu**

is a question-and-answer service designed for K–12 educators. Any question about K–12 education, including staff development, can be e-mailed to AskERIC. A response from a human being will be sent within forty-eight working hours.

Also of interest is the American Library Association's Gopher, launched in mid-April, 1994. The Gopher contains detailed information, including:

- ALA's policy manual

- ALA's constitution

- ALA's bylaws

- schedule of upcoming events

- lists of publications

- staff information, including e-mail addresses

- intellectual freedom statements

- division information

Users may Gopher to

### Gopher://gopher.uic.edu/

Once at the University of Illinois/Chicago Gopher, select the Library option on the main menu, followed by the American Library Association option on the submenu. The ALA Gopher can be directly accessed at:

### Gopher://gopher.ala.org/

The American Library Association also has a WWW home page at:

### http://www.ala.org/

Jamie McKenzie's WWW home page offers a variety of items related to staff development, library futures, planning, and school improvement. One document in particular, *Staff Development for New Technologies*, complements his other relevant papers and publications, many of which are available at:

### http://www.pacificrim.net/~mckenzie/

Media librarians who are beginning to learn about the Internet might consider taking an on-line course for Internet newcomers. Thirty hands-on lessons, distributed over a six-week period, are presented by the Back to School project from the perspective of a media librarian and include on-line information in eight academic subject areas. Back to School can be reached at:

### http://web.csd.sc.edu/bck2skol/bck2skol.html

Another source for on-line courses is ICONnect (Connecting Learners to Information), a three-year technology initiative offered by the American Association of School Librarians (AASL). These courses are designed for media librarians and are offered via a special listserv. To sign up, send an e-mail request to:

### listserv@listserv.syr.edu

Leave the subject line blank and send "Subscribe IBASICS [your first name and last name]" as the message.

Still another Web site that is useful for professional development is the Online Internet Institute (OII). Last year, more than 200 teachers learned on-line, combining hands-on Internet training with follow-up support. The results of these learning experiences are posted at this site, which is maintained with National Science Foundation monies. Visit the OII Web site at:

### http://oii.org

One particularly useful tool that can be used by the media librarian with both staff and students is WebWhacker. This software permits the user to "whack" or retrieve as little or as much of a Web site as wanted and load it onto the hard drive. The user simply provides the URL starting address of the desired Web site and indicates how many levels deep he or she want to go. WebWhacker then contacts the site, downloads each page (including video clips, graphics, and sounds) into a folder on the hard drive, and then relinks the pages. The result is a site that appears the same as if one were surfing live on the Internet. The advantages are numerous, including connect time savings, the opportunity to use the Internet when a modem and telephone line are not available, and the assurance that access to a particular Web site can be guaranteed during an Internet training session. The WebWhacker software may be downloaded (it carries a licensing fee) from:

**http://www.ffg.com/**

## Internet Databases via Telnet

Curriculum information exists in a variety of Internet databases. The Colorado Alliance of Research Libraries (CARL) offers helpful resources and includes on-line text, book reviews, and a database on environmental education. It may be accessed by Telnetting to

**pac.carl.org**

CARL's School Models Program Database contains information that can help media librarians to promote staff development. For example, one model details an interdisciplinary program that highlights the integration of information skills into subject area course offerings.

The Internet can be used to access certain commercial on-line database services such as DIALOG. Instead of using dial-up networks, which can be both time-consuming and expensive, media librarians may Telnet to

**dialog.com**

thereby saving the cost of the dial-up connect time. At DIALOG's welcome screen, the user is asked to log in and enter a password as usual. Once connected, communication with DIALOG's computers is no different from conventional dial-up access.

The Library of Congress catalog can be accessed in several ways. Such access can help the media librarian with cataloging and collection development and can also result in the media librarian's own staff development. Users may Telnet to

**locis.loc.gov**

or, for searching selected portions of the LC catalog, Telnet to

**dra.com**

Data Research Associates provides this service and is not affiliated with the Library of Congress. The catalog can also be accessed via:

**Gopher://marvel.loc.gov:70**

The Library of Congress also provides a wealth of information and resources on the Web at:

**http://www.loc.gov/**

### Reading Lists on the Internet

Media librarians are often asked to provide reading lists for both students and teachers. Many such lists can be found on the Internet. The Children's Literature Web Guide posts lists of award-winning and recommended books, topical bibliographies, lesson plans, and information about authors. It also contains the full text of out-of-copyright children's classics and can be accessed at:

**http://www.ucalgary.ca/~dkbrown/index.html**

# Evaluation and Reflection on the Staff Development Program

**THE ONGOING EVALUATION OF STAFF DEVELOPMENT** for effectiveness and relevance needs constant attention. First, the achievement of staff development learning objectives should be assessed. This can be done in numerous ways and requires participation, reflection, and analysis by the media librarian and the staff development program participants.

Skills to be evaluated can include teacher knowledge of a variety of resources available on the Internet, the ability to access that information for classroom and staff development use, and the integrated and continued use of these resources in curriculum areas. These skills can be evaluated in numerous ways, and the evaluators might use some or all of the following measurement tools:

- portfolios
- journals
- checklists
- rating scales
- anecdotal records
- recorded observations
- conferencing
- peer demonstrations
- interviews
- discussions
- attitude inventories
- surveys
- timelines

Just as a staff development program should reflect the school's mission and philosophy, so should its evaluation. Possible evaluative questions may include:

- Did teachers acquire Internet knowledge and techniques that can be used in the teaching of curriculum units? (If so, how is this being demonstrated?)
- Did teachers experience changes in attitudes toward technology use? (If so, what changes and how are they documented?)
- Did teachers become more comfortable with technology? (If so, how and in what specific ways?)

- Over time, have teachers' behaviors changed in ways that reflect productive Internet use? (If so, what behavioral shifts have been noted?)

Answers to these questions can be reached through the analysis of the information culled from the measurement tools listed. As suggested in chapter 2, quantifiable measures or concrete demonstrations should be used whenever possible. Staff development evaluation, at its most effective, is a reflective, collegial, and cooperative undertaking that results in insightful and positive suggestions for how the program and its instruction can be improved over time.

# Strategies for Diffusion of Faculty Knowledge

**ONCE THE TEACHERS BEGIN** to use the Internet and integrate it into their curriculum areas, they will have success stories to tell. Several of these can help to spread the word about the power of the Internet, as can peer observations. Even some skeptics can be convinced of the Internet's value when they see its productive use in action. Through e-mail, listservs, newsgroups, and postings to relevant Web and Gopher sites, the Internet itself holds great potential for the diffusion of knowledge and exemplary practice.

## Each One Teach One

One particularly effective method of sharing Internet knowledge and encouraging its diffusion throughout the staff is the "each one teach one" concept. This concept, used by Betty Dawn Hamilton, media specialist in the Brownfield, Texas, Independent School District, calls for the media specialist to instruct a number of staff members throughout the year. Each of these staff members will instruct one to three others, who will then in turn teach several others. This system permits the gradual merger of Internet technology into the school, but does not place all of the teaching responsibilities on the media librarian. Such a system also allows staff members to develop and share their newly learned skills and encourages them to become stakeholders in the process of integrating Internet technology into the curricula. A vignette illustrating the "each one teach one" concept appears on the next page.

## Media Librarian as Facilitator

Such a train-the-trainer model needs the media librarian to keep the ball rolling. Media librarians can provide continuing, informal support and assistance to staff members and should be available for collegial planning. They can serve as clearinghouses for Internet updates, share information with other staff members as it becomes available, and serve as mentors and consultants who provide ongoing instruction and support. They can also orchestrate and marshal the school's human resources to optimize mutual assistance and coordinate the flow of Internet-centered information.

Because media librarians communicate with all departments and staff members, they are ideally suited to tracking teacher use of the Internet and what resources teachers are using for their own classroom instruction and for professional growth (subject, of course, to professional privacy). This knowledge enables the media librarian to connect teachers from many departments who can be encouraged to develop interdisciplinary working relationships. Sometimes these connections will extend well beyond the physical boundaries of a school building. Frequently the media librarian will be able to link the skilled with the novice, thus encouraging the practice of peer coaching among teachers and cheerleading for the school's Internet pioneers.

## Staff Development: "Each One Teach One"

Anne Wunderkind, the media librarian at High Tech High School, was excited about the possibilities of integrating the Internet into the school curriculum. The school had about 1,600 students and 140 staff members, and had recently been renovated and expanded. The media center was twice as large as it had previously been and had a networked lab that provided Internet access. Anne believed that access to resources outside of the school could have a positive impact on student learning. She enrolled in a basic Internet course, examined everything she could find about the Internet, and practiced on her home and school computers.

Ms. Wunderkind became comfortable and competent with the Internet. Her next step was to introduce teachers to the Internet and raise their awareness. Along with the expansion project, the high school had also turned to block scheduling, and classes were now held for 90-minute periods. The school administration offered staff development opportunities for teachers to retool and learn new ways to structure student learning during the longer periods. Ms. Wunderkind, a proactive media librarian, saw the opportunity to piggyback Internet training with the other current staff development offerings.

Ms. Wunderkind planned the Internet awareness sessions around department meetings and common planning times, making sure that she highlighted applicable subject areas in the sessions. Once the teachers had some knowledge about what the Internet was, what it could do, and ways in which it might be used in subject areas, Ms. Wunderkind followed up with any teachers who had expressed interest in learning more about Internet technology.

Ms. Spring, a math and physics teacher, indicated that she would be interested in exploring ways to use the Internet in her physics courses. Ms. Spring was especially eager to establish e-mail contacts with other physics teachers and their classes, and wanted to access science information and research from worldwide resources. The school's technology expansion project also provided a two-way fiber optic connection with a local university, and Ms. Spring viewed Internet access as another way for her students to establish links with the science community.

The next step occurred when Ms. Wunderkind and Ms. Spring scheduled multiple Internet training sessions during planning times. Ms. Wunderkind encouraged Ms. Spring to practice and explore and willingly provided support and consultation when needed. Ms. Spring joined a physics resource sharing listserv (**PHYSHARE@psuvm.bitnet.edu**) and established e-mail contact with several members of the physics department at a university.

Ms. Wunderkind and Ms. Spring had frequent meetings that allowed them to talk about newly discovered Internet sites and information and to share the positive (and negative) experiences they had had as they attempted to use the Internet with their students. The two were able to observe each other as they interacted with their Internet-using classes and subsequently met to discuss the observations and give feedback. Ms. Wunderkind and Ms. Spring vigorously publicized new Internet undertakings by sharing Internet teacher achievements and new-found resources with subject-appropriate staff members.

After the multiple Internet sessions, Ms. Wunderkind continued to target and train interested staff members. Ms. Spring, in turn, negotiated new curriculum integration projects with members of the science and math department. Both Ms. Wunderkind and Ms. Spring assumed the roles of Internet consultants and coaches and continued to instruct teachers in the ways of the Internet. The teachers they trained became, themselves, new trainers for their peers. Ms. Spring developed expertise in FTP procedures and gladly helped other interested teachers to master the sometimes-confusing technique; Ms. Wunderkind shared her search technique strategies for accessing remote databases and locating specific information. Newly trained teachers developed other areas of expertise, which they added to the shared skill pool of the school.

## Problems and Possible Solutions

ONCE INTERNET ACCESS AND NETWORKING ARE ESTABLISHED in a school, there is an ongoing need for sufficient technical and support staff to troubleshoot and solve problems. Without adequate networking, equipment, and technical support, implementation will be spotty at best and staff development will be constrained. The initial enthusiasm of pioneering teachers will rapidly wane, and even turn to frustration. These hardware and maintenance concerns should be addressed in the overall technology plan of the school and district.

Adequate time for staff development must be provided to allow staff members to change, develop ownership, and prepare for implementation. Staff development will benefit if a building administrator is supportive and willing to juggle schedules, calendars, and assignment of responsibilities. As McKenzie (1993) pointed out, administrators become good role models by active participation in technology-centered staff development. It is vitally important that time be available for peer coaching (Joyce and Showers 1988). This component is essential to teacher integration of knowledge and skills into the curriculum because it provides ongoing encouragement for the teacher to apply the results of staff development to further student learning in the classroom. Likewise, time must be carved out of the schedule for the media librarian to serve as the teachers' facilitator.

## Summary

THE INTERNET HOLDS GREAT POTENTIAL for providing teachers and students with powerful learning experiences and opportunities. This potential can be unlocked with the leadership of the media librarian. The media librarian may be the most appropriate staff person to become the school's "travel agent," to spearhead efforts to bring the Internet into the school, and to provide staff development for teachers and other staff members. Staff development is a team enterprise. Internet staff development must link with the school and district mission and curricular goals. It should also reflect the content, peda-gogical, and class management development needs of teachers.

Change is a challenge. However, many teachers can be led to new strategies and techniques under the aegis of a well-designed and executed staff development program. For Internet-centered staff development to work, skills in technology and collaborative work must be encouraged. Given the current state of the Internet, it may be most fruitful to work first with those who are curious and eager. The success of the pioneering staff will become a springboard to further involvement with the Internet and, with proper documentation, publicity, and support, will eventually help many other teachers to join a growing community of network travelers.

## Notes

1. *Staff development* refers to continuing education of adults in the context of an employer's mission or goals. The agenda is typically set by consensus of the stakeholders involved; importantly, but not exclusively, by those undergoing the development in question. *Professional development*, in contrast, may emerge more from the personal goals of the individual. These may or may not be con-nected to the institutional mission of the employing organization. The develop-ing professional in such a case may not even be formally employed. In a broad sense, however, anything that enhances the professionalism of an educator will eventually affect the teaching and learning within a school. For that rea-son, the two terms are used interchangeably in this book.

## References

American Association of School Librarians and Association for Educational Communications and Technology. 1988. *Information power: Guidelines for school library media programs.* Chicago: American Library Association/Washington, D.C.: Association for Educational Communications and Technology.

Caldwell, S. D., ed. 1989. *Staff development: A handbook of effective practices.* Oxford, Ohio: National Staff Development Council.

Ellsworth, J. 1994. *Education on the Internet.* Indianapolis, Ind.: SAMS.

Fullan, M., and P. Park. 1981. *Curriculum implementation: A booklet.* Toronto: Ontario Ministry of Education.

Fullan, M., and S. Stiegelbauer. 1991. *The new meaning of educational change.* 2d ed. Toronto: Ontario Institute for Studies in Education/New York: Teachers College Press.

Geisel, T. S. (Dr. Seuss). 1957. *The cat in the hat.* New York: Random House.

Hall, G., and S. Loucks. 1977. "A developmental model for determining whether the treatment is actually implemented." *American Educational Research Journal* 14(3): 263–76.

Honey, M., and A. Henríquez. 1993. *Telecommunications and K-12 educators: Findings from a national survey.* New York: Center for Technology in Education, Bank Street College of Education.

Joyce, B., and B. Showers. 1988. *Student achievement through staff development.* New York: Longman.

Loucks-Horsley, S., C. K. Harding, M. A. Arbuckle, L. B. Murray, C. Dubea, and M. K. Williams. 1987. *Continuing to learn: A guidebook for teacher development.* Andover, Mass.: Regional Laboratory for Educational Improvement of the Northeast and Islands/Oxford, Ohio: National Staff Development Council.

McKenzie, J. (1993). *Staff development for new technologies* [on-line].
>   Available WWW: **http://www.pacificrim.net/**
>   Path: **~mckenzie/**
>   File: **staffd.html**

Metzdorf, J. 1989. "District-level staff development." In *Staff development: A handbook of effective practices,* edited by S. D. Caldwell, 14–25. Oxford, Ohio: National Staff Development Council.

Vandergrift, K. E. 1994. *Power teaching: A primary role of the school library media specialist.* Chicago: American Library Association.

## Chapter 5 ■

# The Internet, School Policy, and the Library Media Program

Schools ... owe it to their children to give them guidance in the self-censorship of materials, the evaluation of resources, and the ethical use of telecommunications.... There are some materials ... [on the Internet] which are not appropriate for children and information which is inaccurate. But just as we would not teach bicycle safety by denying our children bicycles, neither should we teach responsible use of technology by denying children access to it.

*Doug Johnson (1994)*

If Internet use is going to affect student learning, it must be integrated into the school curriculum. Pursuing a vision of improved student learning, however, forces the media librarian and other school personnel to wrestle with some difficult questions. In addition to questions of planning and staff development (see chapters 2 and 4), Internet access raises questions concerning intellectual freedom, censorship, informational gatekeeping, copyright, plagiarism, and student/teacher privacy.

Because each school is unique and must come to grips with these problems in its own way, there will be as many approaches and solutions as there are schools. This chapter enumerates some of those problem issues and provides background material to assist the media librarian and other staff members as they search for solutions to local problems.

# Intellectual Freedom and the Internet: The Issues

## Intellectual Freedom: What Is It?

Intellectual freedom is guaranteed by the First Amendment to the Constitution of the United States. It assures unrestricted access to information and ideas in all communication formats, regardless of the content or the viewpoint of the author or of the person who accesses that information. The two necessary components of intellectual freedom are freedom of expression and freedom to access ideas. Freedoms of action are predicated on intellectual freedom of the mind and thus intellectual freedom is an integral part of American life (Office for Intellectual Freedom of the American Library Association 1996).

Traditionally, the media librarian has had the responsibility of safeguarding such freedoms, while providing print and nonprint materials for student use. Because media librarians are expected to provide both intellectual and physical access to information in all formats (AASL/AECT 1988), the extension of such responsibility to the provision of Internet-accessible information is logical and appropriate.

An excellent source for information on intellectual freedom is the fifth edition of the *Intellectual Freedom Manual* (1996), compiled by the Office for Intellectual Freedom of the American Library Association (ALAOIF). Godwin's essay (1996) provides an overview of freedom of speech and censorship issues in the electronic network and urges people to view electronic networking as an exciting opportunity to participate in free speech and democratic communication. An on-line source is Karen G. Schneider's Freedom Page, a library-related WWW source that links to policy archives, sample policies, banned books, and other pertinent information. This page can be accessed at the following site:

**http://www.intac.com/~kgs/freedom/**

Another on-line source is ICONnect (Connecting Learners to Information), located at the ERIC Clearinghouse on Information and Technology at Syracuse University. In addition to providing a link to information on intellectual freedom, this site provides a wealth of information for media librarians and other educators learning to use the Internet. The home page address is:

**http://ericir.syr.edu/ICONN/ihome.html**

The Gopher address is:

**Gopher://ericir.syr.edu/**

The ALAOIF listserv is yet another on-line source of information concerning intellectual freedom. Sign-up requests should be sent to:

**listproc@ala.org**

## Access

Without informational access, intellectual freedom cannot exist. Access extends to resources outside of the school, including interlibrary loan and computerized information networks such as the Internet. Proper access depends on the media librarian's cultivation of conditions that promote intellectual freedom, such as:

- appropriate media center rules and regulations
- integrated instruction in information skills
- the presence of a sound collection development and selection policy
- solicitation of support when materials are challenged
- positive media librarian and staff role modeling in support of intellectual freedom (Hopkins 1992)

Media librarians need to work with teachers, administrators, and the community to establish and nurture such conditions.

"Access to Electronic Information, Services, and Networks: An Interpretation of the *Library Bill of Rights*" was unanimously adopted by the ALA Council on January 24, 1996, at the 1996 midwinter meeting. The development of this new interpretation took the ALA Intellectual Freedom Committee and other ALA representatives nearly two years and resulted in discussions concerning how librarianship should respond to requests for restrictions on electronic access and information. The interpretation also takes into account the differences in types of libraries and the need for libraries to develop policies based on their unique visions and mission statements. User access and rights, including those of privacy and confidentiality, should be protected, and there should be equity of access to all library users. Parents and legal guardians of minors are encouraged to provide guidance to their own children.

The *Library Bill of Rights* is available from the American Library Association at:

### Gopher://ala1.ala.org/11s/alagophx

"Access to Electronic Information, Services, and Networks: An Interpretation of the *Library Bill of Rights*" can be located via the American Library Association at:

### Gopher://ala1.ala.org/11/alagophx/alagophxfreedom

The document can also be found between pages 48 and 49 of the March, 1996, issue of *American Libraries* and on page 114 of the March, 1996, *School Library Journal*.

ALA's *Free Access to Libraries for Minors: An Interpretation of the Library Bill of Rights* maintains that the right to use a library includes free and equal access to all services, resources, and facilities that are available. Parents have the right to restrict access to library resources for their own children, but do not have the right to restrict other children's access. Librarians have the obligation to ensure equal access to all library users. A copy of the *Free Access to Libraries for Minors* statement can be found at the American Library Association's Gopher site:

### Gopher://ala1.ala.org/11/alagophx/alagophxfreedom

AASL's *Access to Resources and Services in the School Library Media Program* advocates a similar atmosphere of free inquiry and unrestricted access to all media resources and services that are available. A copy of this statement can be located at:

### Gopher://ala1.ala.org/11s/alagophxiii

The user should then select American Association of School Librarians.

## Equity

Equity of access concerns the media librarian deeply. Research on computer-related attitudes and practices in schools has shown that males tend to adopt and use computers more readily than females, and that boys are perceived among peers as more computer-competent than girls (Turkle and Papert 1990). Children from higher socioeconomic groups have superior access to computing and teaching with computers, in their homes and in schools, than do their less affluent counterparts (Picciano 1994; QED 1995).

By themselves, schools cannot remedy the unequal distribution of resources that is ingrained in the inequities of a larger society, but the library media program can pursue initiatives to promote access to technology, including the Internet, for groups that have traditionally been denied that access. This can be done by monitoring the volume and nature of network use within the school, and developing resource banks, curriculum ideas, and inservice opportunities that specifically target underserved audiences, whether by gender, race, behavioral disorder, or disability. Schools and media centers are instrumental in ensuring that students have free, public access to all types of electronic information.

The Internet itself yields information about equity needs and issues. Several documents are available from the Information Infrastructure Task Force at:

### http://iitfcat.nist.gov:94/doc/Education.html

Another good source is *Gender Issues in Computing* by Leslie Regan Shade:

### Gopher://gopher.ncf.carleton.ca/00/ncf/conference/papers/ leslie_regan_shade.txt

## Censorship

By training and intellectual tradition, media librarians tend to resist censorship. The American Library Association (ALA) and the Association for Educational Communications and Technology (AECT) have taken strong, articulate stands against restrictions on access to diverse viewpoints in schools. In *Information Power* (AASL/AECT 1988), opposition to censorship is tempered by a recognition that the selection of school materials should reflect school philosophy, curriculum, and the developmental characteristics of students. Especially considering student developmental needs, the nature of certain Internet-based information poses challenges to schools and the decision-making personnel within them.

**Query and reply posted on the LM_NET listserv, April 17, 1994**

QUERY
```
From:     Lalena Wilber <lwilber@FREENET1.SCRI.FSU.EDU>
Subject: Librarians as Censors
To:       Multiple recipients of list LM_NET
          <LM_NET@SUVM.SYR.EDU>
```
In one of my classes we have been discussing censorship, I was very surprised to discover that a large number of the students in the class seemed prepared to play the role of the censor rather than the protector of intellectual freedom. I was very disturbed by this discovery as many of these students will go on to get jobs in libraries across the country. I was wondering if anyone

else had encountered librarians as censors. And if so how
have you approached them.

**REPLY**

From:     Ken Ponsford <kponsfor@CLN.ETC.BC.CA>
Subject:  Re: Librarians as Censors
To:       Multiple recipients of list LM_NET
          <LM_NET@SUVM.SYR.EDU>
X-To:     Lalena Wilber <lwilber@freenet1.scri.fsu.edu>

Let's not confuse censorship with tailoring the
collection to the clientele. Censorship relates more to
peers preventing each other from having access to
information which each individual should be able to
evaluate for him/herself. Tailoring the collection to the
clientele is always the responsibility of informed adults
who provide for minors.

Two sources for information on censorship issues are:

Internet Advocate Resource Guide
**http://silver.ucs.indiana.edu/~lchampel/netadv.htm**
Internet Resources on Policies and Censorship
**http://www.pacificrim.net/~mckenzie/internet.html**

Debate about pornography on the Internet—particularly, the much-debated Martin
Rimm report on *Marketing Pornography on the Internet* (see Elmer-DeWitt 1995)—
continues. One site, prepared by Donna Hoffman and Thomas Novak, two Vanderbilt
University professors, contains the original article, challenges to the article, Rimm's
rebuttal, and other information concerning the cyberporn debate. This site is the Project
2000 home page at:

**http://www2000.ogsm.vanderbilt.edu/cyberporn.debate.cgi**

In addition to sexually explicit material, students can easily find information that is
incendiary, inappropriate, erroneous, misleading, or unfairly altered. Through staff development, consultation, and direct teaching, media librarians can help teachers and students to
select and evaluate available Internet information and to make informed decisions about
the information's validity. Education in the responsible navigation and use of the Internet
will result in students who are well prepared for learning in the highly technical twenty-
first century.

## Blocking Software: The Search for Solutions

As a result of concerns about offensive items on the Internet, software programs are
being marketed that will permit blocking of Web, Gopher, FTP, newsgroup, and chat channel sites, even if only one explicit source resides there. Because such blocking software
can distinguish only by technical file characteristics, it cannot make value judgments about
informational content. Thus, access to educationally legitimate material at those sites may
be inappropriately denied. For example, the White House Web site was once blocked
temporarily because Socks's (the President's family cat) virtual tour of the White House

contains the word "couples." The use of this word resulted in the blocking of the site until the site's webmaster protested (Salo 1996).

Numerous software products that restrict student access to selected Internet sites are available. These include Cyber Patrol, SurfWatch, Net Nanny, and CyberSitter. LINQ, a complete Internet access solution, is server-based, and Internet access control is one of its many functions and features. Although the specifics of these products vary somewhat, some permit modification of the blocklist to allow or disallow Internet access according to school specifications. A subscription service that regularly updates blocked sites is available, as are multiple-copy discounts and site licensing. One site that lists and describes a number of resources that are available to filter the Internet can be located at:

**http://www.yahoo.com/Business_and_Economy/Companies/Computers/
Software/Internet/Blocking_and_Filtering/**

Other sites that provide useful information concerning such software include:

University of Calgary
**http://www.ucalgary.ca/~mueller/hanson.html**
Internet Advocate Resource Guide
**http://silver.ucs.indiana.edu/~lchampel/netadv.htm**

Discussion of blocking software and the listing of Web addresses for companies that market it do not indicate endorsement of such products. Media librarians are urged to share such information, evaluate it, and then use that information to help their schools make informed decisions concerning the use of such software.

Because of the potential for undue censorship, many media librarians might resist the use of such software. They would argue that although parents may feel a responsibility to place such restrictions on their own children, they lack the right to impose their values on other children. From another viewpoint, however, such blocking software can be seen as a way to regulate access to materials that the school and community perceive as inappropriate in a safe learning environment. Still unanswered are questions such as: What happens if students and parents sign an acceptable use policy (AUP) and the school then uses some type of blocking program? Is the AUP nullified or negated? Is the school responsible for inappropriately accessed materials?

Teaching responsible Internet use and providing careful staff supervision when students are on-line are integral to resolving the problem of student access to inappropriate material. In some situations, however, vigilant supervision might be impossible, for any number of reasons. In these cases, the most practical solution might be staff supervision combined with the installation of blocking software on hard-to-supervise computers (Buchanan 1996). Blocking software will probably not prevent access to every inappropriate site and should not be used as a substitute for education and supervision.

## The Telecommunications Act of 1996

The Telecommunications Act of 1996 was signed into law in February 1996, by President Clinton, who touted the law as enabling the "Age of Possibility." The digitized version of the law was immediately posted to the Internet. One section of the law called the Computer Decency Act, however, is seen by many as a means to control speech and exercise government censorship over Internet content. The act provides large fines and federal prison sentences for those who make indecent words or images available in on-line areas that can be accessed by minors. *Indecency* is vaguely defined, and it is to be measured by "community standards" (never defined). There is also an amendment that prohibits dissemination of abortion information on-line.

Supporters of the act maintain that it will prevent pedophiles and pornographers from preying on children who use on-line resources. The act's detractors maintain that the result will be government censorship, infringement on constitutionally protected freedom of speech, and curtailment of Internet growth and its culture of open access and inclusion. The law is so vague that there is a real possibility that it could restrict the dissemination of educational information. Will educators and schools be liable if a student accesses materials that might fit the vague, broad definition of *indecency*?

The legal ramifications are extensive and, as yet, not clearly defined. The sites listed here will present updated information on this constantly changing legal landscape.

On February 26, 1996, the American Library Association joined a broad-based coalition of organizations (Citizens Internet Empowerment Coalition) in a lawsuit challenging the Telecommunications Act. This case, which will be joined with a lawsuit filed earlier by the American Civil Liberties Union, appears to be headed for the Supreme Court (ALAWON 1996; ALA-led coalition 1996) and a decision on the law's constitutionality. The Coalition has a home page that contains the complaint and background information. It can be located at:

**http://www.cdt.org/ciec/**

Voters Telecommunications Watch, a civic-action group, led a protest against the Telecommunications Act, during which thousands of WWW pages were darkened for forty-eight hours. For current information, the Voters Telecommunications Watch home page can be accessed at:

**http://www.vtw.org/**

Background information concerning the Telecommunications Act of 1996 and its complete text can be located at:

**http://thomas.loc.gov/**

Additional Computer Decency Act information can be found at:

Internet Censorship
**http://www.epic.org/free_speech/censorship/**
Three Rivers Free-Net Computer Decency Act (CDA)
**http://trfn.pgh.pa.us/Internet/Policy/decency.html**

A summary of the Computer Decency Act can be found in *Definitions and Decency* by John S. Quarterman, located at:

**http://www.mids.org/mn/602/def.html**

An uncensored discussion of the law and its potential impact, replete with words that might be deemed inappropriate or offensive to some (browser discretion is advised) can be found at the following HotWired site:

**http://hotwired.com/special/indecent/**

## Establishing a Selection Policy

Clearly, a balance between unwarranted restriction and unfettered access to the Internet is needed. Media librarians have dealt with intellectual freedom issues for a long time. Local conditions may influence local practice, but there is common agreement that a written, districtwide selection and reconsideration policy is needed for all kinds of material.

Such a document outlines the educational objectives of the school, establishes responsibility and procedures for developing a collection, and outlines the criteria that will be used to select materials. It also lays out a stepwise set of procedures to be implemented in response to parent or community complaints about materials in the school. Such a selection policy should include all information formats that are used in the school system, including information accessed via computer networks. For a complete discussion of selection and censorship in schools, as well as sample selection policies, see Reichman's *Censorship and election: Issues and Answers for Schools, Revised Edition* (1993).

*Information Power* (1988) provides additional guidance for intellectual freedom/ selection policy statements. On the Internet, specific selection policies are available from the Electronic Freedom Foundation at:

**http://www.eff.org/**

The *ALA Workbook for Selection Policy Writing* can be found at:

**Gopher://riceinfo.rice.edu:1170/00/More/Acceptable/ selection-workbook.ala**

Media librarians may discover current grassroots thinking on this—or any—subject by posting queries on one or more of several listservs or newsgroups for feedback from colleagues.

# Controls and Informational Gatekeeping

**MOST LIBRARIANS AND TEACHERS** may strive to provide students with unrestricted access to Internet resources, but in actuality some type of staff control and supervision is necessary and desirable. Without the enforcement of basic rules, Internet access could become a chaotic nightmare. Because most students are minors, the school may stand, whether willingly or not, *in loco parentis*. Schools therefore need to take reasonable steps to assure that student Internet use does not exceed the bounds of school rules (a determination that varies from school to school). A well-conceived acceptable use policy (AUP), implemented by media librarians with teacher and administrator support, is essential.

## Establishing an Acceptable Use Policy

Most educational computer networks have acceptable use policies. These policies lay down the conditions under which account holders may use the resources offered. Appropriate and ethical behaviors are outlined, and there is usually a section dealing with consequences for violations. Such a policy must also be flexible enough to cover unforeseen situations. It should stress that use of the computer network is a privilege that carries responsibilities. In most instances, the user is expected to read and sign the policy statement. If a student user is under the age of eighteen, a parent or guardian must co-sign. (What happens if a parent does not co-sign? Is that child somehow identified and denied all Internet access, or just independent access? Can that child participate in a closely monitored class Internet project?) Every school with its own network, or connected to external networks, should develop its own AUP. Because media librarians are well positioned to make informed recommendations about such policies and practice, they should take the lead in doing so.

Acceptable use policies typically cover the following kinds of behavior:

- unauthorized access to restricted data owned by others

- unauthorized manipulation of data owned by others

- plagiarism (not all cases will be as obvious as, say, *Hamlet*, a play, by Murgatroyd Mudflat, Grade 7, Rosencrantz Middle School)

- use of network resources for personal gain (e.g., selling services or products—a practice known as "spamming")

- use of network for illegal or unauthorized activity (e.g., sending of objectionable, obscene, or threatening messages; harassment; downloading of pornographic files; any other illegal activity not specifically mentioned)

- exchange of personal insults (known as "flaming") or unfounded gossip

- intentionally damaging network resources or depriving other users of access to computer resources (e.g., introducing a virus to the network, physically damaging equipment or files, refusing to adhere to standard network procedures)

- excessive network use for recreation (the Internet is replete with games, jokes, and so on, most of them harmless, but to be used in moderation nonetheless)

*Netiquette*, a commonly recognized set of telecomputing courtesies, could be considered as an adjunct to the acceptable use policy. For example, netiquette suggests that: users should check their e-mail frequently and delete old mail; personal messages should not be sent to listservs, bulletin boards, or newsgroups; the subject line should be as descriptive as possible; text postings should not be written all in capital letters because recipients may take it as shouting. Netiquette, however, can be incorporated into an acceptable use policy.

A fascinating case study on acceptable use and what occurs when a fourth-grade student receives obscene e-mail is chronicled in A. Rogers's 1995 *Ballad of an E-Mail Terrorist*. It can be retrieved from the Global SchoolNet Foundation at:

**http://www.gsn.org/gsn/articles/article.email.ballad.html**

Jamie McKenzie emphasizes the need for policies at the school board level, not AUPs. He believes that most AUPs are too limited in scope, as they deal with rules and procedures rather than with broad philosophical and educational issues such as freedom to access information, roles of teachers and parents, integration into the curriculum, and the selection of materials (see the Bellingham, Washington, Web site listed in the next section).

The development of formal access rights and responsibilities provides an excellent opening for media-teacher-community collaboration on teaching about personal responsibility. The benefits of a network are best assured for all when reasonable rules and restrictions are observed. Using the Internet to conduct discussion on relevant issues (such as plagiarism, obscenity, racism, information evaluation, and data theft) can involve students, teachers, and parents in the construction of their own awareness and values about the issues involved. Through listservs, educational databases, and certain newsgroups, sample policies can be downloaded, discussed, evaluated, and synthesized with local realities to develop school policies in which all users have a stake.

## *Acceptable Use: Rich Information Sources*

A sample school acceptable use policy statement can be found in appendix B. Other sample policies and information about writing AUPs can be located at the following sites:

Minnesota Regional Network
**http://www.mr.net/Services/accept_use.html** or **FTP://ftp.mr.net/pub/ MRNet-info/MRNet-AUP.txt**

Texas Education Network
**http://www.tenet.edu/tenet-info/accept.html**

Article by Arlene H. Rinaldi of Florida Atlantic University
**http://www.fau.edu/rinaldi/netiquette.html**

Los Angeles Unified School District
**http://lausd.k12.ca.us/aup.html**

Kings County Office of Education
**http://kings.k12.ca.us/acceptable.use.policy**

Stanford University
**http://rescomp.stanford.edu/use.html**

Armadillo at Rice University
**http://chico.rice.edu/armadillo/Rice/Resources/acceptable.html** or **Gopher://riceinfo.rice.edu:1170/11/More/Acceptable**

ERIC (Educational Resources Information Center)
**Gopher://ericir.syr.edu:70/11/Guides/Agreements**

Internet Advocate Resource Guide
**http://silver.ucs.indiana.edu/~lchampel/netadv.htm**

University of Calgary (Avoiding ethical potholes)
**http://www.ucalgary.ca/~mueller/hanson.html**

Board Policies, Bellingham (Washington) Public Schools
**http://www.bham.wednet.edu/policies.htm** or
**http://www.pacificrim.net/~mckenzie/internet.html**

Consortium for School Networking (information at WWW and Gopher sites is not identical)
**http://digital.cosn.org/** or **Gopher://digital.cosn.org**

Hopkinton (New Hampshire) High School Web Page
**http://www.conknet.com/~hhsweb/library/hhslib.html**

GCCSC (Greenfield-Central Community School Corporation) Board Policy on Internet Use
**http://gcsc.k12.in.us/AUP/AUP.html**

Writing Acceptable Use Policies (Southern Indiana Education Center)
**http://mercury.esc.k12.in.us/aup/1.html**

Another option is to send an e-mail message to:

**info@classroom.net**

and in the body of the message type:

### send aup-faq

*Classroom Connect* will send you frequently asked questions and answers concerning the writing of acceptable use policies for K–12 systems, including a template to use and a list of sites that contain sample policies. The same information can also be obtained via FTP:

### FTP://ftp.classroom.net/wentworth/Classroom-Connect/aup-faq.txt

There are also print sources that will help media librarians to develop AUPs. Among the most useful are:

- Finney's *An Anthology of INTERNET Use Acceptable Policies* (1995)

- *The Internet in K-12 Education* (1993/1994), from the Carnegie Mellon University in Pittsburgh

- Flanders' *A Delicate Balance* (1994)

- Williamson's *Another Look at Acceptable Use Policies* (1996)

The following quotation from a parent underscores the need for an AUP that has parent and community support.

### Acceptable Network Use: One Parent's View
### (taken from the Consortium for School Networking discussion list, July 21, 1994)

```
To:       CoSN Discussion List <cosndisc@yukon.cren.org>
Subject: From a Parent, re: Censorship
```

I'm the PTO President at a small elementary school in rural Minnesota. We have recently installed full, continuous Internet access in each classroom.

Students only have access at the teacher's discretion and under their supervision. They find so many great things to do and see; "inappropriate" use just isn't much of an issue.

I think sometimes we imagine opposition or uproar that isn't there. ". . . borrowing trouble" is what my granddad used to call it.

Prepare an acceptable use policy, talk about it with the students and teachers, bring the issue to your PTO and let them know you are willing to listen to their opinions, then just show kids and parents how wonderful all the quality stuff is—the kids won't have time for the junk.

> Yvonne Karsten,
> PTO President
> Kennedy Elementary School,
> Mankato, Minnesota

## *Security Issues*

There are other situations that even the best acceptable use policy will not easily prevent. Procedures are needed to minimize the potential harm of access by other, unscrupulous Internet travelers to the children in your school. There have been several cases of solicitation of network-using minors by individuals illegally seeking sexual gratification. Schools need not only to regulate and monitor student network access (the younger the student age group, the greater the need for regulation), but also to devise a process for parental awareness building, participation in policy setting, and access permission granting. A potentially useful guide, *Child Safety on the Information Highway*, by Lawrence Magid, can be accessed on the Web at:

**http://www.4j.lane.edu/InternetResources/Safety/Safety.html**

Other sites that contain information on Internet safety can be found at:

University of Calgary (Avoiding ethical potholes)
**http:www.ucalgary.ca/~mueller/hanson.html**
Notes, Advice, and Warnings
**http://www.crc.ricoh.com/people/steve/warn-kids.html**
Child Safety and Censorship on the Internet
**http://www.voicenet.com/~cranmer/censorship.html**

SafeSurf, an on-line organization, is working toward making the Internet safe for children. The group is in the process of developing Internet standards and policies that can be applied to all sites. Eventually, the group is hoping to embed ratings at each site that will be recognized by Web browsers. Parents and schools would then have the option to restrict access to particular sites. For additional information, visit the Web site at:

**http://www.safesurf.com/**

All internal networks have potential security problems that should be identified and resolved. Schools with Internet access must provide an additional layer of security to prohibit unauthorized internal and external access to the Internet (for further discussion on security, see Finney 1995; Varlejs 1996). Options might include keeping Internet access computers in areas that have adequate adult supervision and mandating the use of passwords.

More technologically involved measures should be addressed when the network is being designed. These might include the use of a firewall (hardware and software that permit Internet access while prohibiting intrusions from the Internet), encryption or coding, and biometric devices such as handwriting, fingerprint, and voice pattern recognition (Littman 1996). Littman also outlines the need for the development and implementation of a security policy that will safeguard educational and library/media center resources.

Ongoing vigilance, evaluation, and modification are especially important as new security products and providers appear and make claims of superiority in the field. The media librarian is in a position to be an active participant in such a process and to provide information and synthesis that will allow educators to make informed decisions concerning network security.

# Copyright and Intellectual Ownership

**COPYRIGHT IS NEITHER MORE NOR LESS** than the word implies, the right to copy. Although concrete, recorded expressions of work may be copyrighted, the concepts and theories represented by these expressions may not. The overriding purpose of copyright law is not to reward the producers of intellectual work, but to advance the cause of literary and scientific progress. Copyright law grants to the owner the exclusive right to:

- reproduce
- prepare derivative works from
- distribute copies of
- perform, and
- display the copyrighted work

subject to various exclusions, including "fair use."

## Fair Use of Copyrighted Works

The concept of fair use reinforces the primacy of information dissemination over private right. The unauthorized fair use of copyrighted work is allowed "for purposes such as criticism, comment, news reporting, teaching..., scholarship, or research," according to the U.S. copyright law (17 U.S.C. § 107 [revised 1 February 1993]). The following four practical conditions are considered in defining fair use:

- the purpose and character of the use
- the nature of the copyrighted work
- the portion of the work used in relation to the work as a whole
- the effect of the use upon the potential market for the work.

The term *fair use* is not synonymous with *educational use*. Although educational purpose is a factor to be considered in determining fair use, copyright can be infringed in the service of legitimate educational goals.

By the time the current copyright law was passed, congressionally sponsored committees of users and copyright owners had developed mutually satisfactory fair use copyright guidelines for music, books, and periodicals. Since then, groups of users and producers in other formats (e.g., computer software, video) have cooperatively developed fair use guidelines. These guidelines provide the best available guidance for educational practice.

## Implications for the Media Librarian

In essence, information on the Internet should be treated no differently than information from more traditional sources. It should be treated as the property of the individual or organization that originally posted it. Unless permission is explicitly given, information should not be downloaded, duplicated, or distributed for anything other than one's own personal research. On the Internet, permission requests are easily posted and permission is usually granted. Downloaded information (be it text, image, or other format) should be given proper attribution. Copyright notices should be honored. With or without such notice, the intellectual ownership of others should always be acknowledged.

The subject of copyright may appear dry, but discussion about it can generate an astonishing degree of passion. In the context of economics, ethics, politics, and sociology, the topic offers a rich focus for teaching and learning. Educators talk about the "natural" right of free access to information. Copyright owners stress their rights to the financial fruits of their intellectual labor. In the eye of this hurricane stands the media librarian, for it is the library media program that simultaneously promotes access to educational information and preserves the principles by which such access is governed.

Every school district needs an up-to-date copyright policy, fully sanctioned and supported by practical guidelines. Media librarians are well suited to the tasks of recommending and formulating copyright policy and coordinating school compliance with copyright and information-ownership guidelines. Working from a solid policy foundation, media librarians may take measures to ensure that such policy is respected and observed throughout the school. If schools are serious about teaching citizenship, their personnel should exhibit responsible citizenship through the strict observation of laws, regulations,guidelines, local policies, and commonly accepted ethical standards.

## Help with Copyright: Rich Information Sources

One source of help for media librarians is *Fair Use in the Electronic Age: Serving the Public Interest* (1995), jointly written by representatives of several interested associations. A copy of this document appears in appendix C. Lape (1996) offers a somewhat different view of fair use, however, when she makes the point that fair use should be determined on a case-by-case basis and should not be relied upon as heavily as it is.

There are many excellent sources of copyright information, both on and off the Internet. The *Copyright Primer for Librarians and Educators* (Bruwelheide 1995) is a "must" purchase for all media centers. Another good resource is *Suggested Copyright Policy and Guidelines for California's School Districts* (1991), published by the California Department of Education. Becker's article (1996) provides useful copyright questions and answers, while allowing for additional interpretation and copyright guideline development. Lape, a Syracuse College of Law professor, provides yet another perspective on copyright law and its application in the electronic network environment. She suggests that librarians concentrate too much on protection of material, rather than on the public's interest in accessing such information (1996).

The media librarian can also access copyright information at the following sites:

Copyright Clearance Center
**http://www.openmarket.com/copyright/html/lawinfo.html**

United States Copyright Office, Library of Congress
**http://lcweb.loc.gov/copyright/**

*An Intellectual Property Law Primer for Multimedia Developers*, by J. Diane Brinson and Mark F. Radcliffe (excerpted from *Multimedia Law Handbook: A Practical Guide for Developers and Publishers*, Menlo Park, CA: Ladero, 1994)
**http://www.eff.org/pub/CAF/law/multimedia-handbook**

Copyright FAQ by Terry Carroll, an associate in the Palo Alto, California, law firm of Cooley Godward Castro Huddleson & Tatum
**FTP://ftp.aimnet.com/pub/users/carroll/law/copyright/faq**

Ten Big Myths about Copyright Explained
**http://www.clari.net/brad/copymyths.html**

Copyright Website
**http://www.benedict.com**

Copyright Bookmarks
**http://www.chem.lsu.ed/htdocs/conferences/copyright/copyref.html**

"How Much Is Too Much? Fair Use of Unpublished Materials" by Angie LeClerq at the University of Tennessee-Knoxville
**http://www.lib.utk.edu/utkpubs/infoissues/fairuse.html**

# Ethical Concerns

## Plagiarism

Plagiarism occurs when an author's language, thoughts, or ideas are used without proper attribution, and the resultant work is then passed off as one's own. It is closely linked to copyright and intellectual ownership issues. As with copyright concerns, plagiarism should be discussed with students when they are learning about the proper use of information technology.

Students should be taught the importance of keeping track of where they are obtaining information. When using e-mail, listservs, and newsgroups, students should be encouraged to save information about the original sender and the context in which the message was developed. They should also be cautioned about modification of a message in a way that changes the sender's meaning or misrepresents the sender's identity.

## Proper Electronic Citations

With acceptance of the Internet as a legitimate source of research information, students and researchers need formats for proper citation of Internet resources. As was the case with previously emerging technologies, the standard style manuals did not contain standards for Internet citations and have been slow to respond. Until a commonly accepted form evolves, however, perhaps the most salient points to remember are that citations must be consistent and should provide the reader with enough information to locate the cited information. Guidelines for the citation of works found via the various Internet tools are presented in appendix D.

## Integrity of Student Work

Media librarians can help protect the integrity of student work by discussing the importance of this issue with them and their teachers. If students are going to use the research results of others, or upload the results of their own research to an Internet site, media librarians would do well to:

- urge them to include a copyright notice at the beginning of the work, along with a statement that permits or forbids subsequent copying

- remind them that the content of electronic mail is owned by the originator and that they should seek permission before reposting such messages

- advise colleagues to obtain written student permissions before uploading student work onto any kind of file server

Because the Internet has no centralized supervisory or enforcement authority, each individual network is responsible for policing itself. If students (or staff members) feel uncomfortable with the possibility of losing control over their original work, it may be best to advise them not to upload work onto publicly accessible networks. Such work can be stored on non-networked personal computers.

## Student/Teacher Privacy

Several recent news reports have highlighted situations in which the legitimate privacy of computer communication was breached. Many Internet travelers are not who they claim to be. There are countless opportunities for "private" e-mail messages to be read or altered as they pass through numerous gateways to their ultimate destinations. It appears that "[p]rivacy in the Information Age is evolving into a technological oxymoron" (Carpenter 1996, 41). By keeping up-to-date on appropriate use and security matters and their implementation and enforcement, media librarians can do much to make sure that electronic privacy is maintained to the fullest extent possible.

Although forty-four states, as well as the District of Columbia, have legislated the confidentiality of library records (e.g., circulation data), the Electronic Communications Privacy Act of 1986 (ECPA) is the only existing federal law that deals with e-mail. This law affords privacy protection by prohibiting the interception of private mail that is being transmitted and also prohibits unauthorized intrusion into e-mail that is stored on the system. These two provisions form the legal basis for electronic communication privacy.

There is no current federal law, however, that assures a student's right to privacy when using electronic communication—another instance in which the rapidity of change in technology has outstripped legislation's ability to keep current. Following the lead of several states, Congress is now considering legislation to protect computer data from unauthorized intrusion. The proposed law would make it a crime to break into any computer used for interstate or foreign communication. In a school situation, however, the enforcement of privacy may fall to the media librarian.

It is incumbent upon media librarians (and other staff members as well) to make sure that electronic communication is neither unfairly exploited nor unduly restricted. Having an effective acceptable use policy in place is one of the best ways to safeguard such communication (see prior discussion in this chapter). Although the media librarian is expected to deal with matters of privacy and ethics when teaching about e-mail, users also have an obligation to assume some responsibility for proper use and security of the network and its accounts.

All stakeholders, including teachers, administrators, network administrators, students, and parents, should help shape network security responsibilities. Additionally, the AUP should outline enforcement procedures and penalties that will be invoked for violations. Such a policy will help ensure that students' privacy and due process rights are protected.

The school has the responsibility to provide safe and orderly learning environments. Although students are entitled to a measure of privacy in their electronic communication, when networking they are using school resources for which school personnel are responsible. *Absolute* student privacy can never be guaranteed. If school personnel have reasonable cause to suspect inappropriate network use, investigations by school officials without search warrants may be justified. (For further discussion of privacy concerns, see Finney 1995; Internet in K–12 Education Project Team 1993/1994.)

# Summary

**MANY OF THE ISSUES DISCUSSED** in this chapter defy precise prescription. Because media librarians, other educators, parents, and community members have diverse viewpoints on the issues involved, grappling with them is hard work. There are no simple answers. Instead, local solutions must be carefully, thoughtfully, and collectively crafted by those involved. It is vital that the media librarian be a key participant and a leading problem solver.

# References

"Access to electronic information, services, and networks: An interpretation of the *Library Bill of Rights.*" 1996. *American Libraries* 27(3): between 48–49.

"ALA-led coalition challenges Communications Decency Act." 1996. *American Libraries* 27(4): 13–14.

*ALAWON.* 1996. vol. 5, no. 5, February 26. [ALA-WO listserv] [on-line].
Available e-mail: **ALA-WO@UICVM.CC.UIC.EDU**

American Association of School Librarians and Association for Educational Communications and Technology. 1988. *Information power: Guidelines for school library media programs.* Chicago: American Library Association/Washington, D.C.: Association for Educational Communications and Technology.

Becker, G. H. 1996. "A question of fair use: Copyright and the new technologies." *MultiMedia Schools* 3(2): 30–33.

Bruwelheide, J. H. 1995. *The copyright primer for librarians and educators.* 2d ed. Chicago: American Library Association/Washington, D.C.: National Education Association.

Buchanan, L. 1996. "Surfing in shark-infested waters: Filtering access to the Internet." *MultiMedia Schools* 3(2): 21, 22, 24, 25.

California Department of Education. 1991. *Suggested copyright policy and guidelines for California's school districts.* Sacramento, Calif.: California Department of Education.

Carpenter, C. 1996. "Online ethics: What's a teacher to do?" *Learning and Leading with Technology* 23(6): 40–41, 60.

Elmer-DeWitt, P. 1995. "On a screen near you: Cyberporn." *Time,* 3 July, 38–45.

Finney, P. G., ed. 1995. *An anthology of INTERNET acceptable use policies.* N.p.: National Association of Regional Media Centers.

Flanders, B. 1994. "A delicate balance." *School Library Journal* 40(10): 32–35.

Godwin, M. 1996. "Freedom of speech and censorship in the electronic network environment." In *Safeguarding electronic information,* edited by J. Varlejs. Jefferson, N.C.: McFarland.

Hopkins, D. M. 1992. "School library media centers and intellectual freedom." In *Intellectual freedom manual,* compiled by Office for Intellectual Freedom of the American Library Association. 4th ed. Chicago: American Library Association.

Internet in K-12 Education Project Team. 1993/1994. *The Internet in K-12 education.* Pittsburgh, Pa.: Carnegie Mellon University.

Johnson, D. 1994. *Why Minnesota students need access* [on-line].
Available WWW: **http://www.isd77.k12.mn.us/**
Path: **resources/dougwri/**
File: **why.html**

Lape, L. G. 1996. "A balancing act: Copyright in the electronic network environment." In *Safeguarding electronic information,* edited by J. Varlejs. Jefferson, N.C.: McFarland.

"The *Library Bill of Rights* in cyberspace." 1996. *School Library Journal* 42(3): 119.

Littman, M. K. 1996. "Protecting electronic data: A losing battle?" In *Safeguarding electronic information,* edited by J. Varlejs. Jefferson, N.C.: McFarland.

Office for Intellectual Freedom of the American Library Association, comp. 1996. *Intellectual freedom manual.* 5th ed. Chicago: American Library Association.

Picciano. A. G. 1994. *Computers in the schools: A guide to planning and administration.* New York: Merrill/Macmillan.

Quality Education Data. 1995. *Charts and graphs showing technology implementation in American schools* [on-line].
Available WWW: **http://www.infomall.org:80/**
Path: **Showcase/QED/**

Reichman, H. F. 1993. *Censorship and selection: Issues and answers for schools.* Rev. ed. Chicago: American Library Association/Arlington, Va.: American Association of School Administrators.

Salo, M. 1996, February 21. *Don't you just love it* :-) [publib listserv] [on-line].
Available e-mail: **publib@nysernet.org**

Turkle, S., and S. Papert. 1990. "Epistemological pluralism: Styles and voices within the computer culture." *Journal of Women in Culture and Society* 16(1): 128–57.

Varlejs, J., ed. 1996. *Safeguarding electronic information.* Jefferson, N.C.: McFarland.

Williamson, C. 1996. "Another look at acceptable use policies." *Technology Connection* 3(2): 23, 25.

# Chapter 6

# Internet Made Easy: The Newer Tools

> To someone learning about the Net for the first time, the sheer size can be overwhelming.... I urge you to stick with it, and set your own pace. You alone control your learning process.
>
> Brendan Kehoe (1996)

## Overview

**INTERNET USERS CAN BE EXCITED OR FRUSTRATED** by the variety of resources available worldwide. Curriculum resources abound. Discussion of key issues by educators is lively. Conversations with experts, students, teachers, and librarians in the "global schoolhouse" can be carried on via electronic mail or videoconferencing. On-line resources can be tapped and repackaged for instruction or for administrative planning, requiring only a few steps for most personal computer users. This chapter and chapter 7 present basic information on Internet tools likely to interest media librarians. Some tools, deemed of secondary importance or superseded by more powerful counterparts (a judgment always open to debate) have been left out. These include Hytelnet and WAIS. Information on these and other tools can be found in other sources, such as Ellsworth (1994), Kehoe (1996), Krol (1994), and LaQuey (1994).

Although the traditional Internet tools can be somewhat unfriendly and unforgiving, the situation is improving steadily as hypermedia technology (for example, the graphical user interface browsers such as Netscape Navigator and Microsoft Internet Explorer for the World Wide Web) becomes a presence in school networking. This chapter examines user-friendly World Wide Web tools from the perspective of the school library media program: specifically, the graphical user interface browser Netscape and user-friendly HTML editors. "How to" help is provided, plus the following information:

- search and use strategies for Web resources

- rich resources for educational information

- capturing resources for local use

- publishing information on the Web

- staying current

This chapter also explores videoconferencing on the Internet. Examples of schools using the Internet for real-time contact and shared work are few but growing. Because synchronous communication of this kind will continue to expand, tools such as Cornell University's CU-SeeMe for videoconferencing are addressed, although not treated in detail. The more traditional—and still useful—Internet tools of Telnet, e-mail, newsgroups, and file transfer protocol (FTP) are discussed in chapter 7.

## Netscape, Mosaic, and Lynx: Browsers for the World Wide Web

**ORIGINALLY DEVELOPED IN SWITZERLAND,** the World Wide Web or "the Web" may now be the most frequently used Internet application. As its name implies, the Web is a globally linked aggregation of information that can be accessed through one of several *Web browsers*, tools that understand how to link to and present the information contained on the Web. Each Web location maintains a starting point or overview of its information in a *home page*.

Home pages are created according to a standard format known as *HyperText Markup Language* (HTML). (See figures 6.1a and 6.1b.)

HTML generates formatted text combined with nontext media, such as graphics, sound, and/or video. The user browses a home page and selects an interesting item for further investigation simply by selecting a *hot spot* on the home page. Hot spots may appear as highlighted or colored text, buttons, icons, locations on a map, or other objects; however they appear, they are linked to further information nearby and around the world. In Netscape Navigator for the Macintosh, for example, when the user moves the cursor over the screen, a hot spot is indicated when the cursor changes from an arrow to the icon of a hand. Simply by clicking the mouse while the cursor is positioned on the hot spot, a connection is made to the highlighted item, which can then be explored further.

Web browsers are "hypertext" tools, because they allow users to interact with the hot spots on a page of information and therefore explore information in a nonlinear way. Netscape Navigator is a "hypermedia" tool capable of displaying or presenting all media

&lt;title&gt;Travel Agent: Chapter 7&lt;/title&gt;

&lt;A Name= "Chapter_7"&gt;&lt;H3&gt;Chapter 7 - The Internet, School Policy and the Library Media Program&lt;/H3&gt;&lt;/A&gt;&lt;p&gt;
&lt;HR&gt;

&lt;IMG   WIDTH=150 HEIGHT =150 Align=Right SRC="chapter7.GIF"&gt;

&lt;DL&gt;
&lt;DT&gt; &lt;IMG  Align=Center SRC="gdot.GIF"&gt; &lt;A HREF = "http://www.intac.com/~kgs/freedom"&gt;Karen G. Schneider's Freedom Page &lt;/A&gt;
&lt;DT&gt; &lt;IMG  Align=Center SRC="gdot.GIF"&gt; &lt;A HREF = "http://ericir.syr.edu/ICONN/ihome.html"&gt;ICONnect (Connecting Learners to Information)&lt;/A&gt;
&lt;DT&gt; &lt;IMG  Align=Center SRC="gdot.GIF"&gt; &lt;A HREF = "gopher://ericir.syr.edu/"&gt;AskERIC Gopher&lt;/A&gt;
&lt;DT&gt; &lt;IMG  Align=Center SRC="gdot.GIF"&gt; &lt;A HREF = "http://iitfcat.nist.gov:94/doc/Education.html"&gt;Information Infrastructure Task Force&lt;/A&gt;
&lt;DT&gt; &lt;IMG  Align=Center SRC="gdot.GIF"&gt; &lt;A HREF = "gopher://gopher.ncf.carleton.ca/00/ncf/conference/papers/leslie_regan _shade.txt/"&gt;Gender Issues in Computing&lt;/A&gt;
&lt;DT&gt; &lt;IMG  Align=Center SRC="gdot.GIF"&gt; &lt;A HREF = "http://trfn.pgh.pa.us/policy.html"&gt;Three Rivers Freenet (Carnegie Library)&lt;/A&gt;
&lt;DT&gt; &lt;IMG  Align=Center SRC="gdot.GIF"&gt; &lt;A HREF = "gopher://gopher.eff.org/"&gt;Electronic Freedom Foundation (Gopher)&lt;/A&gt;
&lt;DT&gt; &lt;IMG  Align=Center SRC="gdot.GIF"&gt; &lt;A HREF = "http://www.eff.org/"&gt;Electronic Freedom Foundation (Web)&lt;/A&gt;
&lt;DT&gt; &lt;IMG  Align=Center SRC="gdot.GIF"&gt; &lt;A HREF = "gopher://riceinfo.rice.edu:1170/11/More/Acceptable"&gt;ALA Workbook for Selection Policy Writing&lt;/A&gt;
&lt;DT&gt; &lt;IMG  Align=Center SRC="gdot.GIF"&gt; &lt;A HREF = "http://www.mr.net/MRNet.html"&gt;Minnesota Regional Network (Web)&lt;/A&gt;
&lt;DT&gt; &lt;IMG  Align=Center SRC="gdot.GIF"&gt; &lt;A HREF = "http://gsn.org/gsn/article.email.ballad.html"&gt;Ballad of an E-Mail Terrorist&lt;/A&gt;
&lt;DT&gt; &lt;IMG  Align=Center SRC="gdot.GIF"&gt; &lt;A HREF = "ftp://ftp.mr.net/pub/MRNet-info/MRNet-AUP.txt"&gt; Minnesota Regional Network acceptable use&lt;/A&gt;
&lt;DT&gt; &lt;IMG  Align=Center SRC="gdot.GIF"&gt; &lt;A HREF = "http://www.tenet.edu/tenet-info/accept.html"&gt;Texas Educational Network acceptable use&lt;/A&gt;
&lt;DT&gt; &lt;IMG  Align=Center SRC="gdot.GIF"&gt; &lt;A HREF = "http://www.fau.edu/rinaldi/netiquette.html"&gt;Arlene Rinaldi on Netiquette&lt;/A&gt;
&lt;DT&gt; &lt;IMG  Align=Center SRC="gdot.GIF"&gt; &lt;A HREF = "http://lausd.k12.ca.us/aup.html"&gt;Los Angeles Unified School District acceptable use&lt;/A&gt;

**Figure 6.1a   HTML file shown in Hypertext Markup Language**

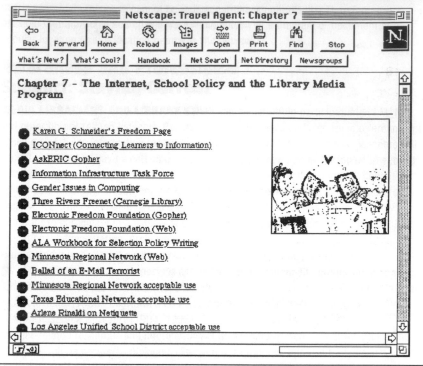

**Figure 6.1b   HTML file shown as Netscape home page window**

*Netscape Communications, the Netscape Communications logo, Netscape, and Netscape Navigator are trademarks of Netscape Communications Corporation.*

types: text, sound, graphics, and motion. Lynx is a hypertext tool that displays only text; when Lynx encounters an image or other media type that it cannot display, it tells the user that nontext information is located there.

Netscape Navigator and its predecessor MOSAIC (hereafter called simply "Netscape") were originally developed at the National Center for Supercomputer Applications (NCSA). Netscape is now available from the Netscape Communications Corporation for most operating platforms. Netscape is an example of a client/server Internet tool, which requires a direct Internet connection or a Point-to-Point Protocol (PPP) or Serial Line Internet Protocol (SLIP) connection. These special connections are more expensive than traditional dial-up terminal/host modem connections.

Lynx is a terminal/host browser that expects commands to be entered from a user's keyboard. Netscape is a client/server browser with a rich graphical user interface (GUI, pronounced "gooey"). Whereas Lynx displays only text, Netscape can present all media types. Both Lynx and Netscape browse the same World Wide Web sites. (See figures 6.2a and 6.2b.)

The main advantage of a hypermedia, GUI browser like Netscape is its ease of use. It is colorful and exciting for all levels of ability and all ages, student and teacher alike. The disadvantage is that its full hypermedia capability imposes substantial system

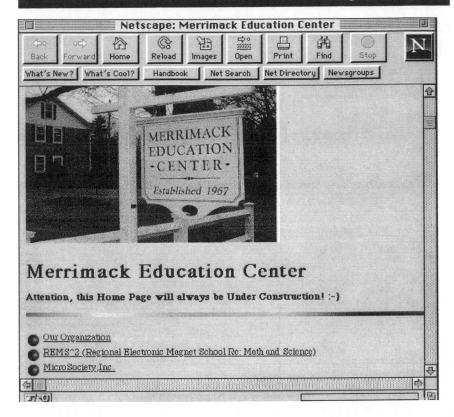

**Figure 6.2a   Merrimack Education Center home page in Netscape**

*Netscape Communications, the Netscape Communications logo, Netscape, and Netscape Navigator are trademarks of Netscape Communications Corporation.*

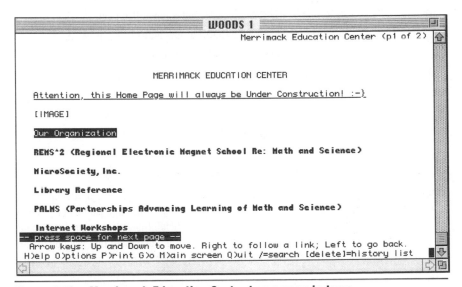

**Figure 6.2b   Merrimack Education Center home page in Lynx**

requirements. Not only must the user have a high-speed connection to the Internet, but the user's system must also be powerful enough to handle multimedia. Most newer computers (Macintosh LC and newer; IBM 386 and newer) have sufficient memory and color display capabilities to support Netscape, but Apple II computers, Macintosh SEs and Classics, and older IBM PCs are best reserved for Lynx browsing.

## Scope and Organization of Information on the Web

Web browsers provide access to Web home pages in addition to other Internet resources found through Gopher, newsgroups, Telnet, and FTP (see the corresponding sections later in this chapter and in chapter 7). Web browsers support Uniform Resource Locators (URLs), which reference resources by the following conventions:

| | |
|---|---|
| http://hostname/filename | Web home pages |
| Gopher://hostname/pathname | Gopher files |
| news://newsgroupname | Newsgroups |
| Telnet://hostname | Telnet databases |
| FTP://hostname/pathname/filename | FTP files |

The prefix "http://" for Web home pages refers to the HyperText Transport Protocol, which indicates that a site maintains a HyperText Markup Language (HTML) home page for access to its information on the World Wide Web. Newer Web browsers also allow the user to send and receive e-mail from within the browser.

A World Wide Web home page is a hypermedia document formatted with HTML tags, which describe how a header is formatted, where an image is placed on a page, how a list of items is displayed, the links indicated by hot spots, and so on. In short, HTML home pages describe the information that a site is making available to users of the World Wide Web and provide references to other files (such as images, sounds, videos, and other files) that constitute the site's published information.

Merrimack Education Center (**http://mec.edu/**), for example, begins its home page (figure 6.2) with a picture (a scanned image) of its main building and then lists its educational programs. Each program is a hot spot, and the user can select any of the program names to learn more. For example, the PALMS program discusses services that MEC provides in its role as a regional resource for the Partnerships Advancing the Learning of Math and Science (PALMS). MEC's innovative PALMS Educational Technology Specialist course has generated an exceptional array of vignettes describing how technology can enhance teaching and learning in math and science across the K–12 curriculum. Included in the vignettes are recommendations for math and science curriculum software.

## Searching for Information on the Web

The "Net Search" button on the Netscape toolbar links the user to a collection of search utilities, including AltaVista, Infoseek, and Lycos. These search engines generally accept a keyword search using Boolean operators (AND, OR, NOT), and allow the user to limit the search results to a manageable number of hits or responses. Search results are posted as a list of resources ordered from most relevant to least relevant. Each item in the list contains a hot spot or link to a Web home page, which the user accesses by pointing and clicking. Some engines, like Infoseek, provide several lines of information about each search result so the user can assess its relevance before linking to the resource. Others, such as WebCrawler, merely give the titles and addresses of the resulting resources.

There are scores of search engines for Web users, many of them represented on the "Net Search" page, and each with its own home page. Each search engine has its own rules for interpreting the user's query, and these rules are generally available to users as "Search Tips" or "Search Hints" on the search engine's home page. For example, the Infoseek search engine, found at:

**http://www.infoseek.com/**

treats capitalized words (proper nouns) different from lower-cased ones. The Search Tips for Infoseek recommend that the user put quotation marks around words in a phrase, hyphenate words that must appear next to one another, and put brackets around words that should appear near one another. Some words in an Infoseek query can be given more or less importance by the user by the placement of a plus (+) or minus (–) sign in front of the word.

Typically, a Web search engine expects the user to enter keywords through a form, which features a long narrow box for the user's typed keywords (see figure 6.3). The user clicks once inside the box to activate it and then types in the query. Several options may be available through nearby menus, perhaps setting the maximum number of hits returned, which operators are to be used, and whether related terms can be substituted for terms in the user's query.

For the sake of comparison, several search engines are described here in greater detail. Lycos, WebCrawler, Yahoo, and AltaVista. The reader should not take this as an endorsement of these search engines. The information is simply indicative of the variety of features and domains for keyword searching on the Web.

Lycos, originally developed by Carnegie Mellon University, claims that its search encompasses more than 90 percent of all Web sites, with about 50,000 documents a day added to and deleted from its "catalog." Lycos is found on the "Net Search" page and can also be accessed directly at:

**http://www.lycos.com/**

Lycos has two methods for adding a document to its database or catalog. Users may register their documents with Lycos. Additionally, a "spider" program scans the Internet automatically and systematically looking for changes to documents and checking new links added to documents in the catalog. The catalog maintained by Lycos includes Gopher and FTP resources.

Generally, a search engine presents the results in order of relevance, with the document judged most relevant first. Lycos measures the relevance of a document (or Web page) to the user's query in terms of how often the document has been accessed by the Internet community. Other search engines may determine relevance by how often a user's query keyword appears in the document. WebCrawler is an example of a search engine that determines relevance by counting the number of times each keyword appears in the document, normalized by the length of the document. Users may experience this as a more accurate search engine than Lycos.

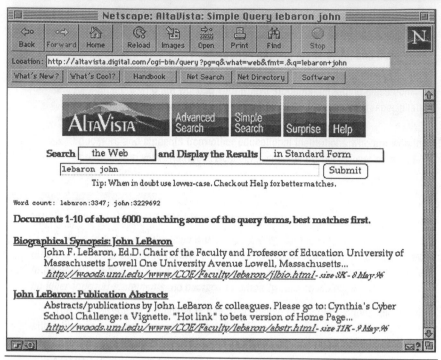

**Figure 6.3   AltaVista search engine**

*AltaVista Search Service courtesy of Digital Equipment Corporation. Netscape Communications, the Netscape Communications logo, Netscape, and Netscape Navigator are trademarks of Netscape Communications Corporation.*

AltaVista is a relative newcomer to the family of Web search engines. Launched by the Digital Equipment Corporation late in 1995, AltaVista is a very large, fast, and powerful WWW search tool. More than 10 billion words in some 20 million Web pages are indexed. Therefore, poorly considered searches may sometimes yield hundreds of thousands of hits. AltaVista accepts quotation-mark strings as substitutes for Boolean searches. Thus, "program evaluation" would yield results only from files with those two words positioned side-by-side. The same two words without quotes would produce hits of pages containing "program" and " evaluation" anywhere in their content. AltaVista can be found at:

### http://altavista.digital.com/

Another approach in search utilities is that found in Yahoo. Yahoo originally provided a directory of information available on the Web, rather than a keyword search engine, although it now includes a keyword search capability. Other search engines are now including a directory approach in addition to their keyword capability. Competition drives continual change in the Web search engine arena! In Yahoo and other directory utilities, users traverse a subject hierarchy, which takes them to relevant pages on the Web. Yahoo is found under the "Net Directory" button on Netscape, as well as the "Net Search" button, or it can be accessed directly at:

### http://www.yahoo.com/

Users who are bothered by the large number of false drops produced by keyword searches in Lycos or Infoseek may prefer to use Yahoo, the best established directory, where intellectual effort has been expended to group relevant pages by broad subject categories. Although recall is lower with Yahoo and other directories than with keyword search engines, precision is higher. Having students explore several search utilities, including Yahoo, is a good lesson in information retrieval.

The University of Twente in the Netherlands posted one of the earliest *meta-search engines* (this one developed by Martijn Kostner), which facilitates searches across a variety of search engines. This "engine of engines" is organized to search information servers, FTP sites, Internet directories, and publications. It is a wonderful single-point launch pad for most kinds of Web searching, and is accessible at:

**http://www_is.cs.utwente.nl:8080/cgi-bin/local/nph-susi1.pl**

More recently, MetaCrawler has arrived on the scene. MetaCrawler, developed by Erik Selberg and Oren Etzioni at the University of Washington, provides keyword access to Web sites. However, it goes far beyond the capabilities of WebCrawler and other keyword search engines by submitting the user's query in parallel to multiple search engines. As of April 1996, a MetaCrawler search encompassed nine engines: OpenText, Lycos, WebCrawler, Infoseek, Excite, Inktomi, AltaVista, Yahoo, and Galaxy. Undoubtedly, others will be added in time. After submitting the user's query to other search engines, Meta-Crawler then collates the results for the user and presents relevant documents, interleaving the most relevant results from the multiple search engines. MetaCrawler is found at:

**http://metacrawler.cs.washington.edu/**

## Rich Resources for Educational Information on the Web

A number of education-related home pages provide good starting points for curriculum and instructional materials, educational discussions, academic resources, and files such as software and clip art. The user connects to one of these sites by clicking on the standard "Open" button on the Netscape window and typing in the URL for the desired home page. Particularly good starting points for professional resources are listed in table 6.1.

One particular Web resource deserves special mention because it is an annotated directory of more than 100 other school-centered leaders in the Internet community, including some of the sites shown in table 6.1. It is the site of Bolt, Beranek and Newman's National Testbed project. Because this is such a dynamic project, its URL changes from time to time. At this writing it is:

**http://copernicus.bbn.com/testbed2/**

Through this directory, contacts and resources may be established with an extraordinary variety of resources, from local school buildings to large national projects and organizations.

Particularly good starting points for curriculum resources include those listed in table 6.2.

**Table 6.1    Professional Resources on the Web**

| Uniform Resource Locator (URL) | Description |
| --- | --- |
| http://www.yahoo.com/Education/ | Yahoo: Education Resources—collection of education resources arranged by discipline (for example, science) or topic (for example, assessment) |
| http://www.ncrel.org/ncrel/sdrs/ areas/gs0cont.htm | Goals and Standards in Education—information about national, state, and local standards for education |
| http://ericir.syr.edu/ | AskERIC Virtual Library—lesson plans, ERIC database and digests, and other high-quality information for educators |
| http://curry.edschool.virginia.EDU/ insite/ | InSITE—International Society for Information Technology in Teacher Education; active discussion on technology in education with pointers to related Web sites |
| http://www.ed.gov/ | U.S. Department of Education—grants, conferences, government publications, and federal initiatives for education |
| http://ics.soe.umich.edu/ | DeweyWeb—clearinghouse for electronic experiential education |

Bringing Internet resources into curriculum and instruction can take many forms:

- Teachers and media librarians can adapt lesson plans or activities they find on the Web

- Teachers and media librarians can download or print materials, such as weather maps, scientific data, word problems, and literature

- Teachers and media librarians can demonstrate Web sites with the aid of a projection device

- Students can explore the Web themselves with any level of structure or supervision

- Students, teachers, and others can publish on the Web

- Students, teachers, and others can be involved in ongoing projects managed through a Web home page.

The Web resources in tables 6.1 and 6.2 give many examples of all of these curriculum activities. Two excellent sources of information about curriculum integration are both from Wentworth Publications: the monthly newsletter *Classroom Connect* and the book *Educator's World Wide Web Tour Guide.* Both resources give concrete suggestions for using specific Internet resources in teaching and learning. *Classroom Connect* is found at:

**http://www.classroom.net/**

*Educator's World Wide Web Tour Guide* is found at:

**http://www.classroom.net/classroom/crctour.htm**

**Table 6.2   Curriculum Resources on the Web**

| Uniform Resource Locator (URL) | Description |
| --- | --- |
| http://www.yahoo.com/Education/ | Yahoo: Education Resources—collection of education resources arranged by discipline (for example, science) or topic (for example, assessment) |
| http://www.mecc.com/ mayaquest.html | Mayaquest Project—educational bicycle trek to the Mayan peninsula, rich in curriculum activities |
| http://seawifs.gsfc.nasa.gov/ JASON.html | The JASON Project—undersea adventures for students, including reef exploration and island formation |
| http://ra.terc.edu/HubHome.html | Technology Education Research Centers—TERC has pioneered hands-on math and science and networking in support of math and science |
| http://www.covis.nwu.edu/ | Collaborative Visualization Project—visual approach to learning |
| http://www.geom.umn.edu/ | Geometry Center—rich math curriculum materials |
| http://web66.coled.umn.edu/ | "Route 66" for Educators on the Web—everything from curriculum ideas to student-created Web pages |
| http://www.exploratorium.edu/ | San Francisco ExploraNet—discovery learning on-line |
| http://ericir.syr.edu/ | AskERIC Virtual Library—lesson plans, ERIC database and digests, and other high-quality information for educators |
| http://www.cs.uidaho.edu/~connie/ interests.html | University of Idaho's "Web as a Learning Tool"—curriculum links and on-line tutorial about developing a home page |
| http://www.capecod.net/Wixon/ wixon.htm | Kathy Schrock's Guide for Educators—great curriculum pointers and educational information about Cape Cod (a good model for school sites!) |
| http://www.gsn.org/ | Global SchoolNet Foundation—projects for Internet schools, ideas, and contacts |

## Bookmarks

Users will find that once they have typed in a complete URL like The JASON Project's **http://seawifs.gsfc.nasa.gov/JASON.html** they will not be eager to retype it. Setting a Netscape "bookmark" is a good way to mark a site for a return visit. Just as one places a bookmark at a favorite passage in any book, so the Netscape bookmark facility allows the user to return directly to a good resource. When the user pulls down the "Bookmarks" menu and selects "Add Bookmark" to mark the current site for a return trip, the site is added to the end of the list of bookmarks at the bottom of the Bookmarks menu. Later, the user simply selects the desired bookmark from the Bookmarks menu and links directly to the resource. Obsolete bookmarks can be removed at any time.

As users find more and more bookmarks, it becomes desirable to organize bookmarks and to exchange bookmarks with other users. "Bookmarks" under the Windows menu provides an interactive capability for both of these activities. The "Bookmarks" dialog box provides tools for sorting bookmarks (up and down arrows for imposing order) and for adding dividers and headers so that bookmarks can be grouped and even placed in submenus with only headers appearing on the main menu. Users can Import and Export bookmarks, and bookmarks can be used on multiple platforms. That is, the bookmarks created and organized on a Windows platform can be imported to a Macintosh, and vice versa.

Bookmarks provide an alternative to keyword or directory searching when the media librarian or teacher wants to guide students to a particular set of resources, rather than allowing them to range freely throughout the Internet. Well-organized bookmarks also provide a simple pathfinder for colleagues new to the Internet.

## Reusing Web Resources for Teaching and Learning

When users find a home page or related file that they want to reuse, they may save an electronic copy or simply print the document. Printing most documents, including images, requires nothing more than pressing the printer icon or selecting "Print" from the File pull-down menu. Text documents can be saved in electronic format by choosing "Save" from the File menu. Images can be saved to disk with one extra step: after choosing "Save" from the File menu, the user specifies that the *format* for the save operation is "Source" rather than "Text."

Some files can be transferred as a whole (downloaded) without the need to display them first, such as application programs or product demos. To download a file, the user simply points at the icon or "clickable" title of the desired file and clicks. A copy of the file is transmitted across the Internet via FTP to the local hard disk (or floppy disk, at the user's discretion). Users are well advised to consider the size of a file before downloading it. Though it might be interesting to have a personal copy of a National Public Radio broadcast, one program could consume 44 gigabytes of storage! The storage capacity of a typical desktop computer would be a small fraction of that.

To read and use files transferred over the Web with still or moving images, sound, or publication-grade formats, appropriate programs will be needed on the receiving desktop computer. For example, the Office of Technology Assessment's book, *Teachers & technology: Making the connection* (1995), may be downloaded via the Web, formatted exactly as it appears in print—illustrations, tables, figures, and all. However, the files for this publication were prepared in a format known as Adobe Acrobat. To read the formatted file, users must have the utility, Acrobat Reader, installed on their local hard disks. The Adobe Acrobat reader can be downloaded from the Adobe Corporation Home Page at:

**http://www.adobe.com/**

Many formats can be displayed directly by Netscape with the addition of helper applications. The Preferences selection on the Options menu allows the user to associate applications such as "Sound Machine" and "JPEG Viewer" with various media types so that Netscape can play or display files with those extensions. More than a dozen media formats are known to Netscape, and the user can add others through this interactive menu item. Figure 6.4 shows an example of the Helper Applications dialog box, focused on two audio and two video file formats.

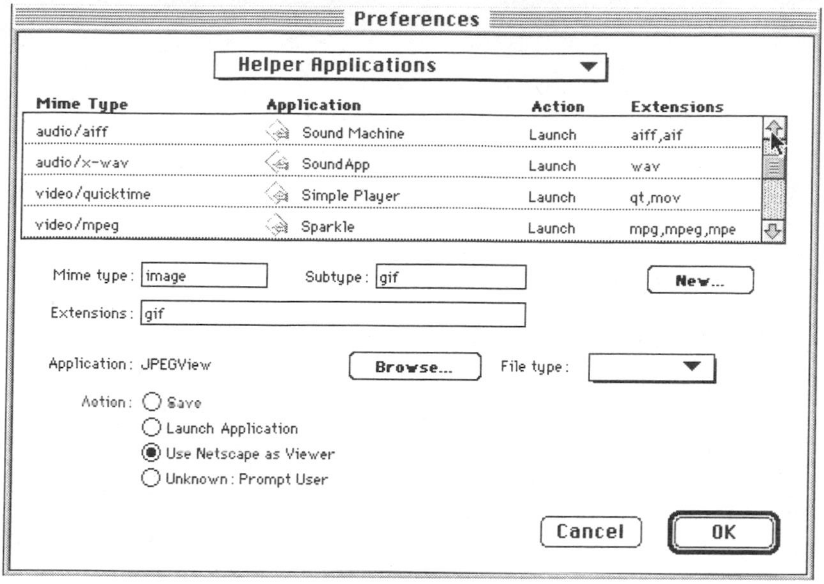

**Figure 6.4　Helper applications dialog box**
*Netscape Communications, the Netscape Communications logo, Netscape, and Netscape Navigator are trademarks of Netscape Communications Corporation.*

When the helper application for a file the user wishes to display or listen to is not already installed on the user's computer (for example, Sparkle, to view a video in the MPEG format), Netscape downloads the file and advises the user that the needed application is missing. The user can save the file for later display or delete it to save disk space. Helper applications are easily located on the Internet by doing a keyword search for the named application. In this case, the user can use Infoseek to look for:

**[Sparkle Macintosh]**

recalling that capitalization tells Infoseek to find only proper nouns and square brackets tell Infoseek to look for words near one another.

The media librarian might assign several students to scour the Internet for helper applications and then make the search results readily available on a network file server or through a set of floppy disks earmarked for that purpose. As users need particular applications, they can quickly install them or ask student helpers to install them.

## Staying Current with the Web

New home pages are added to the Web every fifteen minutes or so. Two standard buttons on the Netscape toolbar link the user to special compendia of new and interesting sites. "What's New" and "What's Cool" are updated at least weekly and provide links to interesting, sometimes outrageous, new home pages—everything from wineries to on-line art galleries and new sources of curriculum materials.

Educators who want to remain current with education-related Web resources may "subscribe" to the listserv "WeeklyB" at

**weeklyb-request@webcom.com**

Reviews of sites that have come on-line over a one-week period can be found at:

**http://www.webcom.com/weekly/**

Selected curriculum sites, reviewed according to structured criteria, are added periodically to:

**http://badger.state.wi.us/agencies/dpi/www/WebEd.html**

# Publishing on the Web

**SCHOOL SYSTEMS AND INDIVIDUAL SCHOOLS** (including individual subject area departments) may choose to create and mount their own home pages. These home pages can be used to promote the values and beliefs of a school, to disseminate information about programs and achievements, to provide a public forum for display of student and teacher work, to establish a link for ongoing projects with other students and teachers (both locally and more globally), and to establish a school's presence. Schools that are competitive in their admissions—for example, independent schools, charter schools, or those engaged in a School Choice program—advertise their capabilities and even provide virtual tours of their facilities via Web home pages.

Home pages are powerful public relations and communication tools that can provide access to students, parents, and other interested parties. School schedules, events, and other relevant information can be posted to the home pages, and assignments and staff e-mail addresses can easily be incorporated. Home pages reach out into the community and permit people to learn more about a school system or individual schools.

Finally, the creation of a home page can provide students with positive, educational opportunities. A home page can be created individually or collaboratively; either way, it requires students to apply what they have been learning. In addition to learning how to make an original HTML file, the students also have to use their higher-level thinking skills to plan, research, organize, and synthesize the information that will be mounted on the home page. Extensive thought and discussion help to determine what the purpose of the home page should be, what the page should contain, how it should look, and whether the end result reflects the original purpose.

Creating a home page for the Web is as simple as creating an HTML-formatted file and convincing a network administrator to make the file available on a Web server somewhere on the Internet. Some commercial services will mount an HTML file for their users for a modest fee. *Classroom Connect* will mount a school home page free of charge on its ClassWeb server:

**http://www.classroom.net/classweb/**

or send e-mail to:

**classweb@classroom.net**

Some schools have their own Web servers, and creating and maintaining Web home pages is part of the curriculum. Hundreds of schools have created their own home pages on the Web. A current listing of schools with Web home pages can be found at:

Web66 School Registry
**http://web66.coled.umn.edu/schools.html**
School Libraries on the Web
**http://www.libertynet.org/~bertland/libs.html**
Peter Milbury's School Library and School Librarian Web Pages
**http://wombat.cusd.chico.k12.ca.us/~pmilbury/lib.html**

Creating a home page is not a complex or highly technical task. An excellent step-by-step guide for library home pages is provided by Garlock and Piontek (1996). On-line documentation abounds for learning HTML and for practicing good HTML style. The Netscape Home Page, at:

**http://home.netscape.com/**

is a good starting point for information about creating home pages, or the user can visit any of the following:

A Beginners Guide to HTML
**http://www.ncsa.uiuc.edu/General/Internet/WWW/ HTMLPrimer.html**
Web Page Design Criteria
**http://www.garlic.com/rfwilson/smalbus/12design.htm**
HTML Quick Reference
**http://kuhttp.cc.ukans.edu/lynx_help/HTML_quick.html**

Finally, Brendan Kehoe's most recent *Zen and the Art of the Internet* (1996) and Ernest Ackermann's *Learning to Use the World Wide Web* (1990) contain excellent reference sections on HTML.

Users can see the HTML that defines any Internet home page by pulling down the View menu in Netscape and choosing "Source." In response to this request, Netscape opens a new window which displays the HTML source file describing the home page it has just displayed. Users can save, print, and edit such source files to create their own variations. The task of creating an original HTML file or editing an existing one is made easier by an abundance of HTML editors, many of which are public domain software or shareware available for downloading. Newer versions of standard word processors, such as ClarisWorks, have HTML editing capabilities.

Some of the more popular shareware HTML editors are available for downloading and simply request that the user register and pay a nominal fee to the developer. Some come with documentation or provide an on-line "Frequently Asked Questions" resource. For example, WebEdit for Windows carries extensive documentation and is available from:

**http://www.nesbitt.com/products.html**

Hot Dog and its commercial equivalent Hot Dog Pro are both described at:

**http://www.sausage.com/**

Users will find that tools such as "Simple HTML Editor," available from:

**http://www.lib.ncsu.edu/staff/morgan/simple.html**

and "Bare Bones Editor," available from:

**FTP://ftp.barebones.com/pub/**

make HTML file creation as simple as using a word processor. That is, one need only high-light the text to be formatted a particular way and choose the corresponding format from a menu. The editor applies the correct tag and then allows the user to preview the change the way Netscape or another browser would interpret it.

To make things even easier, development of a home page can take place on a computer that is not connected to the Internet. The user can even insert links to Internet resources (through a dialog box that is built into the editing tool) and later test the links from a computer that is connected to the Internet. Commercial packages for HTML development, such as PageMill from Adobe, cost less than $100 and come with extensive documentation, extensive features, and tips on sources of graphics and other multimedia resources, as well as telephone support.

# Videoconferencing on the Internet

**ALTHOUGH THE WORLD WIDE WEB** is a vehicle for publishing information to be retrieved by users through a browser, desktop videoconferencing makes it possible to share work and ideas *in real time* with people at remote computers on the Internet.

Traditional videoconferencing is often thought of in terms of elaborate studios with video cameras and high-capacity links to other well-equipped locations. Traditional, room-size videoconferencing costs $100,000 or more, and requires good acoustics, special lighting, and equipment to support and position a video camera and microphone. An interesting on-line tutorial on high-end videoconferencing, including a cost breakdown and illustrations, can be found at:

**http://www.timetool.com/tutor1.htm**

Desktop videoconferencing systems operate on a desktop computer and may use a camera as simple as a $99 QuickCam from Connectix, which looks like a large eyeball attached to the monitor. Utilities like Cornell University's CU-SeeMe software make it possible for anyone with a multimedia computer on the Internet, equipped with a small video camera and a 9600 bps (or better) modem, to communicate "face-to-face" with an educator at a remote computer. Desktop videoconferencing also supports file transfer and shared desktop applications. In short, the desktop computer, outfitted with camera and microphone and linked to a telephone line, is itself the videoconference system.

The basic components of a desktop videoconference system are:

*Input/output.* Input is through a keyboard and mouse, a microphone (sometimes mounted on the user's lapel to cut down on room noise), and a video camera. Output is through the screen image and a speaker and, possibly, through a desktop application such as an electronic whiteboard. Output may also include electronic storage of transferred documents (to floppy or hard disk) or a recording (to disk or VCR) of the session

*Application software.* Makes the connection to the remote user, displays documents and data, and allows interaction with an electronic whiteboard (a virtual surface on which both participants can write or draw and which can be recorded for reuse by other applications).

*Digitizer and compression/decompression (codec)*. Combines multiple input and output streams (sound, image, and data) and compresses them for transmission (or decompresses received signals for display).

*Communications network*. Internet or private data network using telephone lines or other network facilities.

*Macworld*'s 1994 review of four desktop videoconferencing systems (Leeds 1994) explored four desktop systems ranging from $1500 to $6,000 and noted that most have poor sound quality (sometimes not even equivalent to speakerphones) and vary widely in image quality. However, desktop videoconferencing is affordable and manageable in the classroom. There are also alternatives to videoconferencing that provide a shared whiteboard without video and sound. These systems include Face to Face from Crosswise and Vis a Vis from World Linx. A survey of desktop videoconferencing products can be found at:

**http://www3.ncsu.edu/dox/video**

General information is available at:

**http://www.yahoo.com/Computers/Multimedia/Videoconferencing/**

Educational uses of desktop videoconferencing may involve students directly in curriculum-related activities or may be targeted to staff development. A lively discussion of educational uses of videoconferencing, including examples and case studies, is on-line at:

**http://www.kn.pacbell.com/wired/vidconf/Intro.html**

David Thornburg (1994) also provides practical approaches to using teleconferencing effectively in a school environment.

Some schools are engaged in desktop videoconferencing via the Internet, many of them through the Global Schoolhouse Project or Global SchoolNet:

**http://www.gsn.org/gsn/cu/index.html**

The Global SchoolNet provides a restricted-access "reflector" or channel for interactive videoconferences with multiple parties. This restricted-access reflector can be scheduled by schools that do not want to risk having their educational activity interrupted by uninvited guests.

The technology used by Global SchoolNet and other schools is a public domain desktop videoconferencing system developed by Cornell University (CU) called CU-SeeMe (pronounced "See You, See Me"). This chapter does not presume to explain CU-SeeMe. An excellent discussion of the software, the underlying technology, and its application in education is provided by Tim Dorcey in *Connexions* (1995) and is available at:

**http://cu-seeme.cornell.edu/DorceyConnexions.html**

Educators interested in remote "face-to-face" communication are encouraged to learn more about CU-SeeMe public domain software from the CU-SeeMe home page at the following Web address:

**http://cu-seeme.cornell.edu/**

This Web site also features pointers to further information about small video cameras and audio capabilities that support desktop videoconferencing without a high price tag. The CU-SeeMe home page also hosts discussion lists and event guides, and even has T-shirts.

CU-SeeMe software and documentation for the Macintosh and Windows platforms may be downloaded free of charge from:

**FTP://CU-SeeMe.cornell.edu/pub/CU-SeeMe**

# Summary

**THE NEWER INTERNET TOOLS**—Web browsers, HTML editors, and desktop videoconferencing—provide exciting and challenging opportunities for media librarians and their schools. Graphical user interface browsers such as Netscape bring the full multimedia capability of the Internet into classroom and research activities. Schools can mount their own home pages to showcase student work, promote their educational philosophies and programs, establish on going projects, and provide a forum for professional communication. Students and educators can interact in real time through desktop videoconferencing, providing lively communication of ideas and information.

Chapter 7 discusses traditional Internet tools, which have enduring value, especially for schools that do not yet have multimedia computers with high-speed connection to the Internet.

# References

Ackermann, Ernest. 1996. *Learning to use the World Wide Web.* Wilsonville, OR: Franklin, Beedle & Associates.

Dorcey, T. 1995. "CU-SeeMe desktop videoconferencing software." *Connexions* 9(3) [on-line].
Available WWW: **http://cu-seeme.cornell.edu/**
File: **DorceyConnexions.html**

Ellsworth, J. H. 1994. *Education on the Internet.* Indianapolis, Ind.: SAMS.

Garlock, K. L., and S. Piontek. 1996. *Building the service-based library Web site: A step-by-step guide to design and options.* Chicago: American Library Association.

Kehoe, B. P. 1996. *Zen and the art of the Internet: A beginner's guide.* 4th ed. Upper Saddle River, N.J.: Prentice-Hall.

Krol, E. 1994. *The whole Internet user's guide and catalog.* 2d ed. Sebastopol, Calif.: O'Reilly & Associates.

LaQuey, T. 1994. *The Internet companion.* 2d ed. Reading, Mass.: Addison-Wesley.

Leeds, M. 1994, November. "Desktop videoconferencing." *Macworld* 87–92.

Office of Technology Assessment, U.S. Congress. 1995. *Teachers & teaching: Making the connection.* Washington, D.C.: Government Printing Office.

Thornburg, D. 1994. "Why wait for bandwidth?" *Electronic Learning* 14(3): 20–23.

# Traditional Internet Tools

> This may be an Information Superhighway,
> but I'm in the breakdown lane with a flat.
>
> *High school science teacher*

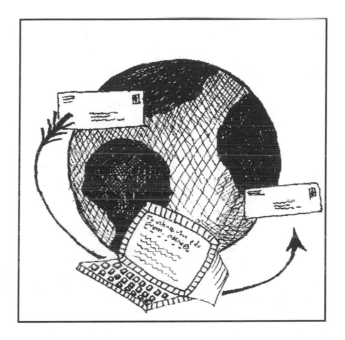

Some schools do not yet have the high-speed Internet connection and multimedia-equipped computers to take advantage of the newer applications. For those who must make do with slow dial-up modem connections to Internet hosts or with older personal computers, there is still a wealth of information. Some users of older computers and slower connections may have access to Unix-style Gophers and Lynx WWW browsers. Others, however, may not. These users will need to navigate with the Internet's traditional tools: Telnet, newsgroups, and FTP (file transfer protocol). Virtually every Internet traveler will use electronic mail, regardless of local computing power or telecommunication set-up.

# Gopher

**GOPHER IS A VERSATILE TOOL** for browsing and retrieving information from Internet sites around the world. Gopher is easy to use and presents a very simple menu interface to the user. For schools enjoying high-speed Internet access from multimedia computers, Netscape or an equivalent Web browser may be the preferred gateway to Gopher. Some schools may not have such a browser, however. For these Internet accounts, Gopher offers an appealing alternative. As more and more users hook up to the WWW, however, Gopher services may gradually close down, with time-tested resources being transferred over to Web servers.

## Scope and Organization of Gopher Resources

The Gopher domain is organized in multiple menu layers called *GopherSpace*. Gopher menus point to a vast array of resources. Although these resources may include sound, images, and video, Gopher can only present text documents correctly on the screen. Image, sounds, and other nontext resources (such as images that conform to the Graphical Interchange Format or GIF) can be downloaded for later use by programs that can interpret their formats (such as GIFconverter). Gopher allows users to view text documents on screen, to e-mail them, and to download (save) files locally.

Some newer Gopher clients are able to access Web resources on the Internet by launching a Web browser at the appropriate command. Gopher can also fetch FTP resources (see the related sections later in this chapter). Software and other encoded files can be downloaded from certain FTP archives; Gopher will decode many such files. Through its menu structure, Gopher will make Telnet connections. Many excellent Telnet sites, such as NASA Spacelink and Teacher Pages, are accessible from Gopher menus. Gopher's ability to handle FTP and Telnet functions makes it possible for novice Internet users to explore these resources without having to remember Telnet addresses or deal with the cumbersome unfriendliness of FTP commands.

Users may wonder how GopherSpace is organized, hoping there is some equivalent of the Library of Congress Subject Headings and a comprehensive on-line Subject Index for Gopher resources. There is not. However, there are a few secrets to successful Gopher searching. The geographical index to Gopher servers, the alphabetical list of Gopher servers, a list of subject-specific Gophers, and a short lesson in how Gophers are created are helpful on-line aids for users. These are outlined here.

The "Mother Gopher" at University of Minnesota offers a hierarchical geographic index (in menu form) to Gopher users worldwide. This is a useful starting point when a user hears about a remote Gopher server but does not know its address. Users can navigate quickly through continents, countries, regions, and states to an individual Gopher providing resources germane to a particular need.

Users often find new avenues to explore when they peruse the alphabetical list of "All the Gopher Servers in the World" or "Gophers Servers in the US," both of which are found in the geographical index. The lists contain hundreds of Gophers, and the lists change frequently, but it is worthwhile to have a printout of the list handy for those with Unix-style Gophers (text-based, command-driven clients that present menus as numbered lists). Knowing a server's approximate number in the multiple-screen listing makes it easy to home in on that particular Gopher for exploration.

Many Gophers are devoted to one subject or area of interest—the environment or chemistry, for example. If we consider that most Gopher servers in the world have been developed in specific response to the needs and interests of a particular community of users, it becomes apparent how Gophers are organized:

- Each Gopher server provides a number of local resources for retrieval that are unique in GopherSpace.

- Links can be made to a particular resource from any menu to another menu anywhere in GopherSpace.

- The set of menus for a particular Gopher features pointers and links to resources that its community is interested in. Some of the resources are local and some are remote.

This organization suggests that the best Gopher search strategies are to:

- make use of Gophers that cater to interests similar to the user's (such as education-related Gophers and subject-specific Gophers)

- explore Gophers at schools and institutions that specialize in the user's interests, such as Brown University for women writers or Woods Hole Oceanographic Institute for marine biology

- use keyword search tools, such as Veronica, to search across GopherSpace (see the discussion of Veronica later in this section)

- explore book and document collections—library catalogs, journal databases, and electronic books and journals

- explore archives of listservs in the user's area of interest

- make use of bookmarks (see "how to" discussion later in this section) to resources not readily available on the client menu, and share bookmarks with others who have the same interests

## Gopher Use and Search Strategies

Gopher resources are uniform. They do not depend on the operating system of the user's computer. However, the user interface to Gopher may differ from one computer to the next. Personal computers directly connected to the Internet via direct high-speed connection (or by dial-up access using a PPP or SLIP service at 14,400 bps or faster) may use the point-and-click environment familiar to Macintosh and Windows users. The Gopher in this environment is often called a *Windows-style* Gopher. Some users, however, must use a slower dial-up modem connection to an Internet host, and the Gopher interface available to them consists of menus with numbered choices. Users of this *Unix-style* Gopher indicate their choices by typing the number of the desired item (or moving a cursor with the arrow keys) and pressing the <return> key. Gopher commands are given by typing a single letter (not followed by pressing <return>). Figures 7.1a and 7.1b show a Turbo-Gopher and a Unix-style window for the main Armadillo Gopher directory. This Gopher was created by students and teachers of the Houston, Texas, Independent School District.

Several Gopher commands are particularly useful. Table 7.1 provides Windows-style commands from the Macintosh TurboGopher interface, along with the equivalent command from the Unix-style gopher interface. Certain Unix-style commands ("print" and "save," for

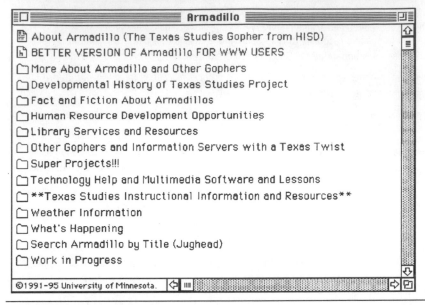

**Figure 7.1a   Main Armadillo Gopher directory shown in TurboGopher window**

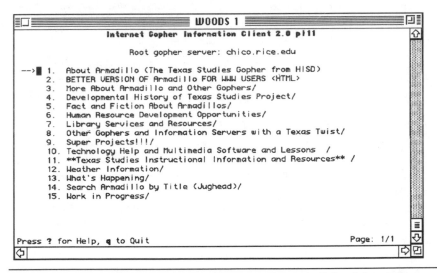

**Figure 7.1b   Main Armadillo Gopher directory shown in Unix-style window**

**Table 7.1    Gopher Commands in Windows and Unix**

| Action | TurboGopher 2.0 (Macintosh) | Unix |
|---|---|---|
| Connect to another Gopher | Gopher/Another Gopher... | o |
| Return to previous menu | Close window | u |
| Print document | File/Print | *** |
| Save document | File/Save as... | *** |
| Mail document | [not available] | m |
| Obtain reference (path) information | Gopher/Get Attribute Info & URL | = |
| Set a bookmark | Copy/paste menu item or folder to a Bookmark Worksheet | |
| Show bookmarks | Gopher/Show Bookmark Worksheet | v |
| Save (export) bookmark file | File/Save Copy as Bookmark Worksheet | *** |
| Read (import) bookmark file | Gopher/Open Bookmark Worksheet | *** |

example) depend on the capabilities of the communication software that supports the connection to the Internet host. Those commands are marked with three asterisks (***) and are explained in the following discussion on capturing resources.

As in Lynx or Netscape, Gopher bookmarks provide a convenient way to return directly to an interesting resource without the user having to remember the path taken when the resource was originally discovered. Bookmarks can be saved as separate files and exported or imported for use in colleagues' Gopher clients.

*Veronica* is a Gopher search tool that looks for user-entered keywords. Veronica maintains an index or database for its GopherSpace searches. Veronica's database represents most Gopher servers and provides keyword access to Gopher directories and titles in directories. Naming practices in GopherSpace are strictly nonstandard. As a result, a keyword search in Veronica may produce several false hits and may miss some pertinent resources.

Veronica is used by selecting it from a Gopher menu and supplying keywords in response to a prompt. Once the user gives a keyword or keywords, Veronica searches its indexes and presents the results in the form of a Gopher menu. The menu can be used like any Gopher menu, and items of interest can be bookmarked, printed, saved, read, or mailed like other Gopher menu items.

Combining keywords in a Veronica search can produce more accurate results. Users can combine terms by giving natural-language phrases or Boolean operators (AND, OR, NOT). Phrases are interpreted by Veronica as keywords combined with AND. Thus, "portfolio assessment" is equivalent to "portfolio AND assessment". Veronica ignores upper and lower case and does not care about the order of the terms. Users who want to broaden a search may want to use OR, but, as Steven Foster explains in his "How to Compose Veronica Queries" (usually available from the same Gopher menu as Veronica), searching with OR tends to "produce thousands of hit-or-miss results. 'OR' is best used in conjunction with other operators." In the portfolio example, the user might want to search for "portfolio AND (management OR assessment)".

The wildcard (*) is a valuable feature of Veronica. When users are searching for "fractals" or "aquifers," for example, material may be titled with the singular or the plural. A wildcard "fractal*" or "aquifer*" will find both, but using the singular or plural form alone will only turn up exact matches to the singular or the plural. Wildcards are allowed only at the ends of terms.

Veronica searches can be restricted in other ways, besides keyword combinations. Users can limit the search to the type of resource desired—sound, image, text, Telnet connection, and so on. The list of options is found in Foster's document, which is a standard item on most Gopher Veronica menus. Another useful document on the same menu is the current " Frequently Asked Questions (FAQs) about Veronica."

## Rich Education Sources on Gopher

The following are good Gopher starting points for curriculum and instructional resources and materials on educational issues:

- Armadillo (**Gopher://chico.rice.edu:1170/**). A wide range of educational resources created by students and teachers in the Houston, Texas, Independent School District.

- AskERIC (**Gopher://ericir.syr.edu**). Syracuse University's repository of ERIC resources, similar to those available via the AskERIC WWW site. Includes keyword ERIC searching, lesson plans, AskERIC Q&A service, ERIC digests.

- The Best of K-12 (**Gopher://gopher.ties.k12.mn.us**). Minnesota's Technology and Information Educational Services school consortium. Offers materials for teaching and learning; information about networking.

- Consortium for School Networking (**Gopher://cosn.org** See also **http://cosn.org**). Includes educational, technical, and policy-related information about school networking and related issues.

- Education Gopher at the Florida Institute of Technology (**Gopher://sci-ed.fit.edu**). Features curriculum materials in several disciplines and gateways to electronic books.

- Empire Internet Schoolhouse (**Gopher://nysernet.org:3000/11**). New York State's regional Internet gateway. Provides curriculum materials. Of special interest to school personnel is the "Academic Wings" folder.

- National School Network Testbed (**Gopher://copernicus.bbn.com/** See also **http://copernicus.bbn.com/testbed/**). Bolt, Beranek and Newman's national project advancing school reform through networking. Includes curriculum resources, educational software, references to other resources, and more.

- U.S. Department of Education (OERI) (**Gopher://gopher.ed.gov**). Contains information about federal education legislation, grant news, conferences, and links to other resources.

## Capturing Gopher Resources for Local Use

Saving a Gopher document on a personal computer is a two-step process for users who are dialed into the Internet in a terminal/host arrangement. When an interesting document is found, the user gives the "Save" command ("s"). Once the Gopher session is over, the user initiates a file transfer between the Internet host and the user's personal computer. Often, this transfer is accomplished with Kermit, or a similar protocol, which is "spoken" by most popular communication packages and by Internet hosts. Typically, the user gives a Kermit command to the Internet host, indicates which file to send, and then commands the communication software on the personal computer to receive the Kermit file. Details on transferring files (FTP) appear later in this chapter.

Printing a Gopher document from a Unix-style Gopher is as straightforward as issuing the "Print" command ("p"), unless the user is dialed into an Internet host where the printer is in a different location. When printers are not accessible, a document can be downloaded and then FTPd to a computer with a printer available. When printers are available, it may still make sense to FTP the file to the desktop computer connected to a convenient printer. As an alternative, users may display and highlight the document, and then choose "File/Print Selection" from the menus provided by their communication software. For long documents (more than one screen), the user should begin highlighting at the end of the document and scroll backward. Printing and saving Gopher files are good methods for applying relevant Gopher resources in educational settings.

## Staying Current with Gopher

Users can normally rely on their favorite Gophers to keep up with new additions to GopherSpace in their areas of interest. Announcements of new Gophers and new resources (such as ERIC digests) are posted regularly in Net_Happenings, CoSNDISC, LM_Net, and other listservs. Users will also see references in literature and hear about new resources at conferences and through word-of-mouth. Resources found through citations should be bookmarked if they prove to be worth a return trip.

# Simple E-mail

**ALTHOUGH THE WWW PROVIDES ACCESS** to richly mediated information sources, electronic mail (e-mail) is the keystone of personal communication on the Internet. E-mail connects students with subject experts, students with other students, and teachers and librarians with colleagues around the world. Because of its accessibility and ease of use, e-mail is the tool of choice for many school projects. As Bragg (1995: 6) points out, e-mail "is probably the most commonly available and most frequently used service of the Internet." It is the basis for on-going discussion on listservs (see discussion of listservs and newsgroups later in this chapter).

Every individual with an account on an Internet-connected computer has an e-mail address, and can therefore send and receive mail quickly to or from any other addressee. System requirements are minimal. Considering that the Internet comprises 35 million computers in almost 150 countries (Internet Society 1995), even in its simplest configuration, e-mail is a powerful tool. Many business cards include e-mail addresses as data no less important than telephone and fax numbers and conventional mailing addresses. For many teachers, e-mail is an excellent starting point for using the Internet. The media librarian often takes the lead in getting teachers to apply for accounts and begin using e-mail.

## Organizing and Forwarding Messages

Once users have received a dozen or more mail messages, the media librarian may be called on to help organize messages and to manage information overload. A handout on the commands for creating folders or directories, suggestions for naming, and commands for deleting messages will be useful at this time.

When passing messages to colleagues, users may extract portions of them or eliminate the lengthy headers (which, on some older systems, give the history of a message's path from Internet source to destination). Some e-mail systems prohibit editing a forwarded item, because editing would change the integrity of the original message. In unusual circumstances, this restriction may be circumvented by saving (or extracting) the body of the message and then editing the resulting document as the basis of a new, edited message. Such editing should be done rarely. When changes are deemed necessary, the forwarder should indicate that there were changes and provide reasons for making them.

## Sources of Internet E-mail Addresses

Users will also want to know how to find Internet addresses. Some networks have internal address books on a Gopher server, and these are helpful. Over the years, the Internet has been a notoriously poor directory of user names and addresses. Beyond the individual network, newer, more responsive "people directories" are appearing, but there are still no universal, reliable, searchable databases of Internet users. For starters, user directories such as WhoWhere (**http://www.whowhere.com/**) or WHOIS (**http://www.intellinet.com/CoolTools/Whois/** or Telnet to: **rs.internic.net**) are worth a try. Better approaches for finding Internet addresses, however, might be:

- Contact the person directly and ask for a current Internet address.
- Look for Internet addresses on business cards.
- Look in biographical summaries in WWW home pages, at the ends of journal articles, or in conference proceedings.
- Get an address from mail that individuals have sent or from postings they have made to a newsgroup or listserv.
- For college or university personnel, consult the Gopher at the person's campus and look for a directory of faculty and staff.
- If the Internet host name is known, send a username query to the system postmaster.
- "Finger" the Internet node (if its name is known) for likely usernames (e.g., surname "friel" preceded or succeeded by first initial "lfriel" or "friell," or first name_surname, "linda_friel"). This operation will not work very well for nodes that use obscure naming procedures for their account holders.

A Finger command to another Internet location will usually list the usernames of current logons. This command may also confirm the account of a current user. For an outside Internet user guessing (correctly) that the University of Massachusetts Lowell generally uses a surname/first initial nomenclature, the following Finger query to WOODS.UML.EDU for co-author Linda Friel produced the following report.

```
$ finger friell@woods.uml.edu
[woods.ulowell.edu]
Login name:FRIELL  In real life: Linda Friel
Directory: DCE_FAC$DISK:[FRIELL]
Last login:1-OCT-1996 11:50:18
Has no new mail.
Forward: MRGATE::AM::FRIELL
```

# Listservs

**MANY INTERNET USERS** use e-mail for purposes other than one-to-one private correspondence. They may join one or more e-mail distribution lists. Many of these lists began
as "BITNET listservs." BIT (Because It's Time) NET is a network of academic and research
computers, and access to it is possible via Internet e-mail, enabling participation in BITNET
e-mail lists. *Listservs* are electronic mail distribution lists set up by associations of network users dedicated to electronic discussion on a countless variety of topics. Besides the
BITNET listservs, several other e-mail distribution list types also can be found on the
Internet (e.g., listproc, majordomo, mailserv).

Users subscribe to listservs in the users' areas of particular interest. Once subscribed, electronic mail is distributed to everyone on the list (membership size ranges from
the tens to the thousands of users). Mail can be directed to individual list members, but to
do so *that particular* person must be explicitly and individually addressed. Embarrassing
mistakes can be made when the originator of a message, believing that a message is
being directed to only one other user, is actually broadcasting to hundreds or thousands.

To join a listserv, one typically sends mail to a program named "listserv" at the
address where the list is administered. (For CoSN, the program is "listproc"; for the Global
Schoolhouse, it is "lists"; for others, it may be "majordomo" or "mailserv".) The recipient
of the subscription request is often a program; therefore, the request must follow an exact
format. The subject line may be left blank. The body of the message is usually one line
with the following words:

### SUBSCRIBE name-of-list your-first-name your-last-name

Here is an example (using VAX/VMS mail) of subscribing to the PACS-L listserv:

```
To:    "listserv@uhupvm1.uh.edu"@inet
Subj:  SUBSCRIBE PACS-L Kate Collier
```

Once you belong to a listserv, you can send mail to the list (for example, PACS-L) by sending a message thus:

```
To:    "PACS-L@uhupvm1.uh.edu"@inet
Subj:  my message
       Kate's words of wisdom on a topic ...
```

Notice that you *subscribe* to "listserv," but you *send contributions* to "PACS-L."

When you want to get off the distribution for a listserv, send a message to the listserv
program (not to the list!) saying you want to UNSUBSCRIBE:

```
To:    "listserv@uhupvm1.uh.edu"@inet
Subj:  UNSUBSCRIBE PACS-L
```

There are countless listservs dedicated to many K–12 topics. Ellsworth (1994) and
Miller (1994, 1995) provide extensive directories of them. Listservs can be wonderful
tools, but they can also overwhelm a user's electronic mailbox. Users simultaneously
subscribed to KIDLINK, IECC, and EDTECH, for example, could receive more than 100 messages per day. Messages occupy personal disk space. It is wise to subscribe only to listservs of obvious value, and to unsubscribe if the value becomes dubious. Users may want

to browse the archives of popular listservs (available through AskERIC and other education Gophers and home pages) before deciding to subscribe.

Listservs, or e-mail distribution lists, of special appeal to media librarians, teachers, and instructional technologists include:

**COSNDISC@list.cren.org**
Coalition for School Networking (discussion on school-based computing with emphasis on networking)

**CU-SEEME-SCHOOL@gsn.org**
Global Schoolhouse (information on Internet-based videoconferencing)

**EDTECH@msu.edu**
Educational Technology (general)

**IECC@stolaf.edu**
International education/cultural exchanges

**KIDLINK@vm1.nodak.edu**
Foreign language projects

**KIDLIT-L@bingvmb.cc.binghampton.edu**
Children's literature

**LM_NET@listserv.syr.edu**
Library-Media discussion (the *premier* list for school media librarians)

**MEDIA-L@bingvmb.cc.binghampton.edu**
Media in education

**NETTRAIN@ubvm.cc.buffalo.edu**
Training strategies for Internet

**PACS-L@uhupvm1.uh.edu**
Public Access Catalog Systems Forum

Alternatively, users may want to join a listserv with the option of not receiving mail, then use the archives to follow the discussion and simply mail in a question or response when needed. If an archive for a particular listserv is not current enough or if several favorite listservs are not archived, the media librarian might serve as the designated subscriber for several listservs, or might encourage several active teachers to share responsibility for a number of listservs. This eases the burden on any one individual and promotes collegiality.

Individual users often create several of their own personal distribution lists for smaller groups of people with whom they work on particular projects. Assuming that the list members read their e-mail regularly (and their participation is of little value if they do not), personal distribution lists offer a highly effective way to turn around information within work groups of various size quickly and efficiently. A personal distribution list is similar to a very small listserv, but it differs inasmuch as other account holders cannot mail to the personal list.

There are thousands of listservs. Finding the right ones can be a challenge. Often-times news about noteworthy e-mail lists comes through personal colleagues or professional associations. TileNet (a service of the Walter Shelby Group) offers a well-organized, interactive directory of Internet e-mail list services, with the capability of subscribing directly from their Web site. Directories of newgroups and FTP sites are provided as well. TileNet is located at:

**http://tile.net/**

An excellent listserv user's guide appears on the Web at:

**http://www.earn.net/lug/notice.html**

# Newsgroups

**NEWSGROUPS ARE SIMILAR BUT NOT IDENTICAL** to listservs. They serve as discussion forums for people interested in a wide variety of topics. As distinct from e-mail lists, however, Internet users do not need their own personal subscriptions to read, post, reply to, and follow up on newsgroup messages. Moreover, newsgroup postings do not occupy scarce disk storage allocations on each user's personal account. Some e-mail lists are "mirrored" as newsgroups, but many are not.

Thousands of newsgroups exist. Most of this growing number were started and maintained by a loose coalition of USENET members. The roster changes every day as new newsgroups come into being and old newsgroups discontinue operation. Individual users need access to a "newsreader" client that allows access to newsgroups. Such clients may allow users to select particular newsgroups that will appear on a "registration" menu in the newsreader whenever it is fired up. Registration in this case does not bestow personal membership, as does subscribing to a listserv. Rather, it simplifies matters in that users need only deal with the small number of preferred newsgroups for which they have registered. The newer Web browsers are featuring newsreading client capability.

Newsgroups are classified by a hierarchical naming structure. A newsgroup name generally consists of two or three identifiers connected by dots (for example, "**comp.internet. library**"). The leftmost identifier signifies the kind of newsgroup, and the rightmost the specific group. Newsgroup classifications include: "k12" (school issues), "rec" (recreation), "talk", "sci", "comp" (computers), "bit" (BITNET listservs), and so forth. One particular classification, "alt", hosts unclassified groups. Some of these are obviously inappropriate in public school settings (such as "alt.adults.only"), and offer a persuasive argument for judicious supervision of student Internet activity.

As an aid to the selection of useful newsgroups, the University of Massachusetts Amherst makes available *The Ednet Guide to Newsgroups*, a categorized list of groups particularly relevant to educators. This list may be retrieved as a file from the university's public access FTP site either via the WWW or by the more arcane FTP process outlined later in this chapter (**FTP://nic.umass.edu/pub/ednet/ edusenet.gde**). Other newsgroups that media librarians and teachers may find useful include:

alt.education.distance (distance education/learning)

bit.listserv.aect-l (educational and instructional technology)

bit.listserv.axslib-l (library access for the disabled)

bit.listserv.edtech (educational technology: general)

bit.listserv.pacs-l (public access library catalog systems)

comp.internet.library (electronic/virtual libraries)

k12.ed.tech (educational technology: schools)

k12.library (school library media issues)

misc.education.multimedia (as the newsgroup name implies)

Newer newsreaders and e-mail programs are enhancing the power (and the potential risks) of these seemingly humble tools (Putzel 1995). It is now possible to insert WWW hot links into a newsgroup posting. E-mail utilities, such as the ones found on Netscape and Microsoft Internet Explorer, allow interactive links, programs, *and viruses* to be embedded into simple messages. The benefits are obvious. In an e-mail message, hot pointers can take the reader to relevant network resources or to educational files produced by the sender. By the same token, messages from unknown sources can create malicious havoc and distribute inappropriate information to computers and storage devices used in schools. The lesson is that increased networking power requires more professional care.

# Telnet

**THE TELNET** (or remote login) tool enables users to log in to Internet computers other than their own. Many remote hosts maintain information databases for public use, available through a Telnet connection. Some Internet services provide users with a separate Telnet tool, whereas others allow access to Telnet sites through Gopher or the World Wide Web. On a Web browser, the URL format for a Telnet resource is

**Telnet://hostname**

Once a Telnet connection is established, the user must log in using a legitimate username recognized by the remote host. Generally, each Telnet database has an associated "guest" or "public" username and password. When such a database is announced for public access, the information includes:

- address of the remote host
- username (if any) for use by guests
- guest password (if any)
- any other information necessary for successful login

Once logged into the database, users must deal with the remote computer's interface. The bad news is that there is no uniformity among interfaces to Telnet databases. The good news is that most interfaces provide necessary navigational help at login, with information about such critical operations as how to get help and how to log out.

Users should be encouraged to print out or jot down this information before proceeding. Nearly all remote systems will have "help" commands. These are typically activated by typing "Help", "H", or "?" while logged into the remote system. A good strategy when accessing a help file during a Telnet session is to print the on-line help instructions when they are provided.

Telnet users should be aware of the universal panic button, the "Control-Close" command. Pressing the Control key and typing the right square bracket "control-]" will usually break a Telnet connection cleanly and return users to their home computing environments. This command is particularly useful when the interface is unmanageable or when the database seems to "hang" or remain unresponsive for several minutes.

Some of the available Telnet resources are invaluable, especially for educators without access to the World Wide Web. For example, library catalogs may be searched through a variety Telnet sites. In some cases, the full text of articles and other documents may be ordered on-line.

Some popular Telnet resources for educators are:

- Cleveland Freenet/The Schoolhouse-Academy One. Provides a national platform for school-centered network projects, including access to library resources and electronic discussion forums (host **Telnet://freenet-in-a.cwru.edu**, **Telnet://freenet-in-b.cwru.edu**, or **Telnet://freenet-in-c.cwru.edu**).

- Colorado Alliance of Research Libraries (CARL). Offers a variety of document search tools and further Telnet links to library catalogs nationwide (host **Telnet://pac.carl.org**).

- Library of Congress Information System. Connects users to the LC Gopher server, offering public access to LC catalogs and files. Includes rich information about current legislation and copyright (host **Telnet://marvel.loc.gov**. Log in as "marvel"). This service can be accessed by a Gopher client.

- National Aeronautics and Space Administration (NASA). Provides updated text, images, and sound-based information on current space explorations (host **Telnet://spacelink.msfc.nasa.gov**; username "guest").

- UMassK12. Provides access to Telnet, Gopher, and newsgroup sites of particular school interest, in addition to local bulletin boards. Various on-line library catalogs may be searched through UMassK12 (host **Telnet://k12.ucs.umass.edu**. Log in as "guest").

- Weather Underground/University of Michigan. Provides weather conditions and forecasts for all regions of the United States (host **Telnet://downwind.sprl.umich. edu 3000**).

Telnet capacity is a boon for academic travelers. With temporary access to any Internet computer in the world, educators may make a Telnet connection back to their home computers, without paying long-distance telephone charges, and perform work as they would at their own offices.

# FTP

**FILE TRANSFER PROTOCOL** (FTP) is one of the oldest Internet information retrieval tools. Developed and perfected by engineers in the days of ARPAnet as a means of sharing files for research or military purposes, the basic FTP tool still looks like the no-window-dressing operation that it has always been. "Traditional" FTP tools are able to move files of any size and type on a global scale with speed and integrity, but they are not user-friendly. Because many FTP resources can now be accessed via Web browsers and Gopher menus, it is easy to give up on FTP after initial trials end in frustration. For experienced Internet users, however, FTP is powerful. Also, because some FTP files are still not accessible from Gopher or the Web, veterans will continue to use this tool.

For Macintosh platforms directly connected to the Internet, Fetch (a GUI navigational interface) offers a simpler point-and-click tool for transferring remote files. A Windows equivalent is called WS_FTP. In general, these GUI tools make a connection to an FTP site and allow the user to browse the remote directory structure as though it were a collection

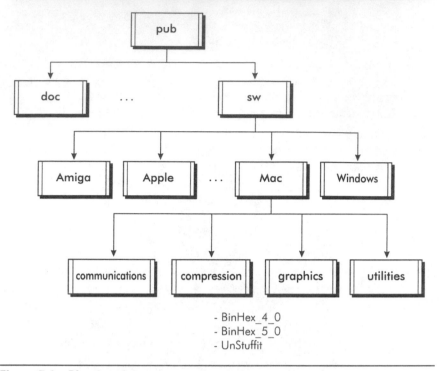

**Figure 7.2    Directory tree**

of file folders. Fetch and WS_FTP simplify the selection and retrieval of files, and handle decoding and decompression of many retrieved files automatically and transparently.

The directory structure for FTP archives is a "tree." A typical directory tree for the public files on an FTP site might look like the structure in figure 7.2, where "pub" indicates publicly available files, "doc" indicates text documents, "sw" indicates software programs, and so on. Naming conventions assist users in finding files in FTP archives. The "sw" subdirectory is typically subdivided into directories such as "amiga", "apple", "msdos", "mac", and "windows" for various platforms. As explained later, the terms "Bin Hex" and "UnStuffit" refer to the systems used for coding and compressing the files stored at public FTP sites.

Copies of key directories are often "mirrored" on systems with large file storage facilities in various geographical regions. Examples of files likely to be mirrored are public domain software (such as Kermit and Netscape) and documents for Internet administration.

There are several essential principles to keep in mind for successful FTP use:

- To retrieve a file using FTP, the user must know the host name and the path. The Archie search tool can help with this (see the section on Archie later in this chapter).

- FTP sites reorganize their directories occasionally and leave pointers to new locations of files that have been moved. In this case, the "Change Directory" (cd) commands allow the user to navigate up and down the directory tree.

- *FTP is case-sensitive!* ("MAC", "Mac", and "mac" all read differently in FTP mode.)
- Although many files are ASCII-encoded, it is important to watch for non-ASCII-encoded files and treat them as "image" or "binary."
- The file extensions (".hqx" ".cpt" ".zip" and so on) inform the user what encoding and compression tools have been applied to the file. The user should be ready with the corresponding software tools for decoding and decompressing the file once it has been retrieved (for example, Bin Hex for ".hqx" files; UnStuffit for ".sit" files; CompactPro for ".cpt" files; PKunZip for ".zip" files). Many of these public domain utilities are available from public FTP archives.
- Some files are self-extracting. These files are designated with the ".sea" suffix and, when downloaded to the client computer, will decode and decompress automatically. They are ready to be used when the downloading is done.

The most useful commands for FTP users are those for making a connection, obtaining on-line help, navigating the directory tree, and retrieving files. These commands are represented in the following table:

| Command | Action |
| --- | --- |
| open **hostname** | Makes a connection to the FTP site named **hostname** |
| help | Shows the commands available at the FTP site |
| dir | Displays a list of files and directories |
| cd **pathname** | Changes the directory to the directory specified by **pathname**. *This is the command for navigating the directory tree* |
| cd .. | Moves back up one level in the directory tree |
| get **filename** | Retrieves the file named **filename** |
| close | Ends the connection to the FTP site |
| exit | Terminates the FTP session |

Old-fashioned FTP is not recommended for the novice educator. However, it holds potential value for the media librarian as a tool for retrieving public domain software and resources, which can be examined and evaluated for possible inclusion in the local software collection. From an instructional standpoint, the variables associated with file transfer present interesting problem-solving exercises for students to tackle: transfer rates; best times to make connections for transferring large files; cost/benefits of high-speed modems; managing file storage space during decoding and decompression of large files, and the like.

The library media program may wish to consider training a cadre of "Internet Scouts" (students especially interested in technology) to assist with retrieving public domain software for evaluation and use in the district. FTP archives at the University of Michigan, Stanford University, University of Washington, and Dartmouth College maintain vast stores of public domain software, organized by function, suitable for use on Macintosh, Apple, DOS, and Windows platforms. The steps for retrieving such packages are:

1. Locate a copy of the software through Archie (see explanation later in this chapter) or by browsing through directories of software archives.
2. Connect to the host and navigate to the correct directory.

3. Transfer the file to the user's Internet host and disconnect from the archival site.

4. Using Kermit or a similar downloading protocol, transfer the file from the Internet host to a personal computer.

5. Check the file for viruses (this is important!).

6. Decode and decompress the file (Fetch and WS_FTP may perform these functions automatically).

7. Check the file for viruses again (some virus checkers cannot detect a virus until the file has been decoded and decompressed).

8. Check the documentation and perform a trial launch of the package.

Once the technical side of the downloading task is done, the media librarian might then:

1. Organize a demonstration for interested teachers.

2. Assist teachers in using and evaluating the package.

3. If teachers make a decision to use the package in their teaching, add it to the school's software collection.

A file that is added to the software collection usually includes documentation concerning the file's origin, how it can be installed and run, and any restrictions that govern its use. This information is often presented in a README document associated with the software, and this document should be read carefully before downloading or using the software. Information in the README files should be shared with teachers and students who become subsequent users.

## FTP Archives for Curriculum and Teaching

- Dial-up access and ideas for Internet use by libraries (**FTP://dla.ucop.edu**). ALA-sponsored publication of library resources.

- *Incomplete Guide to the Internet* (**FTP://ftp.ncsa.uiuc.edu** Directory: **Education/Education_Resources/**). The National Center for Supercomputing Applications on-line Internet guide; may be dated.

- Telecomputing in schools (**FTP://ftp.tapr.org** Directory: **pub/ed-telecomputing/ telecomputing-info**). Tucson Amateur Packet Radio's (TAPR) cornucopia of resources on school networking, including many older but insightful documents written by Judi Harris.

- Ames Research Center SPACE archives. (**FTP://explorer.arc.nasa.gov** Directory: **pub/SPACE/**). Educational resources from the National Aeronautics and Space Administration.

- Images for K-12 use, in GIF format. (**FTP://ftp.tapr.org** Directory: **pub/ed-telecomputing/telecomputing-info/gif-gallery**). More educational resources from Tucson Amateur Packet Radio.

- A comprehensive collection of FTP sites for educators. (**FTP://ftp.tapr.org** Directory: **pub/ed-telecomputing/telecomputing-info/IRD/ IRD-ftp- archives.txt**). Still more information from TAPR.

# Archie

**JUST AS VERONICA IS A TOOL** for searching GopherSpace by keyword, Archie is a keyword tool for searching FTP archives. Developed at McGill University, Archie (short for "Archive") is a database query system for the thousand-plus anonymous FTP sites worldwide. Archie servers maintain databases of FTP sites and directories for public archives. Normally, an interactive Archie session is initiated either through a local Internet Archie client (if one is available) or by remotely logging in to an Internet site housing an Archie database server (see list later in this section). Alternatively, Archie is available as a menu item on many Gopher menus along with popular FTP sites. Users who do not have access to tools other than e-mail can initiate an Archie search by sending an e-mail request to

**archie@archie_server**

(see the following for a partial list of Archie server sites) with the simple word "help" in the body of the message. The return message will explain how to frame a particular search.

Typically, Archie sessions are launched by making a Telnet connection to an Archie server. At the login prompt, the user responds "archie." No password is needed. At the main prompt, the "help" command will provide clues about how Archie works and how the database can be searched. Issuing the "prog" command with a keyword generates a search for files containing the keyword. The more specific the keyword (for example, "MacKermit" as opposed to " Kermit"), the more precise the results. The search results display the FTP site address, the directory path to the file, the filename, and other attributes of the file.

Archie server sites include:

- archie.sura.net (Maryland)

- archie.unl.net (Nebraska)

- archie.rutgers.net (New Jersey)

- archie.internic.net (New York)

- archie.au (Australia)

- archie.doc.ic.ac.uk (England)

- archie.ac.il (Israel)

- archie.nz (New Zealand)

Archie maintains a database for keyword access to filenames and directories on known, public FTP archives. Users may wonder if Archie queries *every* site that supports FTP. The answer is no. At the time of an Archie search, the Archie server handling the search makes an FTP connection with each of the FTP sites currently represented by the database and looks through the directories represented by the database for all matches between the query and the files currently maintained in those directories. The search is dynamic, but it only covers known sites and known directories—those represented in the current Archie service database. Further, if an FTP site is not available at the time of a user's search, its response cannot be included in the search results. Therefore, it is possible that an Archie search will not turn up a copy of a program or document at a popular location or at a location nearby in the network.

## Awareness and Professional Support: Staying Current

**MEDIA LIBRARIANS AND LIBRARY STAFF** can benefit from participation in LM_Net and other library-related listservs. Perusal of library catalogs and electronic reference databases may provide information regarding valuable material for acquisitions. Teachers will benefit in the same way by participating in listservs and newsgroups germane to subject areas or topics of interest. Exploration of tools like Netscape and Gopher will benefit all school personnel. Administrators are likely to need syntheses of educational issues on short notice. They should be directed to AskERIC for ERIC digests on the issue. They may also want to participate in a listserv such as K12ADMIN, which addresses current issues in educational administration. Archives of the listserv will provide an overview of discussion to date, and a well-placed question may bring useful support and ideas.

Three other books are especially rich in their presentation and organization of educational resources on the Internet. These are Wentworth Publishing's *Educator's World Wide Web TourGuide* (1996), Ellsworth's *Education on the Internet* (1994), and Miller's *The Internet Resource Directory* (1994, 1995). The central clearinghouse for all kinds of Internet-related resources and information will be the library media program. There, the resources will be secured, cataloged, discovered, distributed, and used. As discussed in chapter 4, staff development for Internet infusion throughout the school is most appropriately orchestrated in the library media program.

## References

Bragg, C. A. 1995. *Summary of Internet resources* [computer printout]. Waltham, Mass.: Bentley College.

*Educator's World Wide Web Tour Guide*. 1996. Lancaster, PA: Wentworth Worldwide Media.

Ellsworth, J. H. 1994. *Education on the Internet.* Indianapolis, Ind.: SAMS.

Internet Society. 1995. *Global and country level domains of the world* [on-line]. Available WWW: **http://info.isoc.org/** File: **domains.html**

Miller, E. B. 1994, 1995 update. *The Internet resource guide for K-12 teachers and librarians.* 1994/1995 edition. Englewood, Colo.: Libraries Unlimited.

Putzel, M. 1995. "Like getting an e-mail bomb." *Boston Globe*, 22 September.

# Sample Pathfinder for Internet Staff Development

Tho following pathfinder is an example of several that were developed to be used during a workshop to help teachers learn to use the Internet. It will help teachers to find lesson plans and learning activities that can be used in the classroom and connected to the curriculum. As the teachers follow the path, they will travel through a number of different sites that can be explored in future visits. This one was designed by Thomas Kane, Principal, Annie L. Sargent School, North Andover, Massachusetts.

The pathfinder begins with the main menu of Mass Ed Online LearnNet. The first five steps should be modified if a different network is used.

### Pathfinder 1 (K–3)

My Reduce/Reuse Story Activity
Curriculum Area: Science

This pathfinder will bring you to a lesson that integrates science, language arts, and art around the theme of environmental awareness. The lesson is in a site called EE-LINK, the Environmental Education Gopher, which includes a range of resources on environmental educational programs for Grades K–12.

1. At the main menu, select *Massachusetts and Worldwide Resources* and press <return>.

2. At this next menu, select *Mass Department of Education* and press <return>.

3. Next, select *Connect to DOE Gopher* and press <return>.

4. At the DOE menu, select *Other Information Service* and press <return>.

5. Next, select *Other Education Gophers* and press <return>.

6. At this menu, select *EE-LINK, the Environmental Education Gopher*, and press <return>.

7. Once in EE-LINK, select *Solid Waste-Cornell* and press <return>.

8. Next, select *K-3 Activities* and press <return>.

9. Finally, select *My Reduce/Reuse Story Activity* and press <return>.

The journey through this pathfinder brings you through some interesting intersections where you can explore other resources that may be useful in your classroom program. At step 6, the menu for Other Educational Gophers offers many other avenues to explore where you will find resources for all areas of the curriculum. Also, at step 7, you can search through an extensive collection of activities related to environmental education.

# Sample Acceptable Use Policy

The Nueva School in Hillsborough, California, is a private prekindergarten–8 school. Its acceptable use policy ties into the school's library selection policy and reflects the American Library Association's position papers about access for minors. To provide the parents with information to perform their role, free parent Internet training is provided. This is not, however, another "how to use e-mail" class. Instead, the class reviews the acceptable use policy, selection and censorship issues, Internet resources, and the curriculum. The policy was selected for inclusion here because it presents the necessary information in a clear, concise, and nontechnical way.

## NuevaNet Acceptable Use Policy and Contract

### *NuevaNet MISSION STATEMENT*

NuevaNet is a service provided by and in consonance with the dual mission of The Nueva School:

*Mission I: To enhance innovative education for gifted and talented children through access to unique resources and collaborations;*

*Mission II: To improve learning and teaching through research, teacher training, collaboration and dissemination of successful educational practices, methods, and materials.*

NuevaNet is connected to the Bay Area Regional Research Network (BARRNet) which in turn connects it to the Internet. The Internet links computer networks around the world, giving NuevaNet access to a wide variety of computer and information resources. In general, electronic traffic passes freely in a trusting atmosphere with a minimum of constraints.

NuevaNet provides open access to these local, national and international sources of information and collaboration vital to intellectual inquiry in a democracy. In defining the Internet's resources as an extension of the Library, this network subscribes to the Library Bill of Rights which states that "A person's right to use a library should not be denied or abridged because of origin, age, background or views."

In return every NuevaNet user has the responsibility to respect and protect the rights of every user in our community and on the Internet. NuevaNet account holders are expected to act in a responsible, ethical and legal manner, in accordance with the Nueva Code of Conduct, the missions and purposes of the other networks they use on the Internet and the laws of the states and the United States.

### NuevaNet ACCOUNT HOLDERS

A NuevaNet account is a privilege offered each academic year to the following:

1. All students at Nueva, prekindergarten through grade eight, and their parent(s) or guardian(s).

2. All educators who are working with Nueva students, including classroom teachers, support personnel, administrators, tutors, music staff, specialists and mentors.

3. Educators and students from other educational institutions who are working in partnership with The Nueva School for specific purposes over a limited period of time.

### NuevaNet CODE OF CONDUCT

NUEVA's Code of Conduct applies to all users of NuevaNet. It reads:

*"I will strive to act in all situations with honesty,integrity and respect for the rights of others and to help others to behave in a similar fashion. I will make a conscious effort to be of service to others and to the community. I agree to follow Nueva's basic rules: no killer [hurtful] statements, no damage to property, and no violence."*

The NuevaNet account holder is held responsible for his/her actions and activity within his/her account. Unacceptable uses of the network will result in the suspension or revoking of these privileges. Some examples of such unacceptable use are:

1. Using the network for any illegal activity, including violation of copyright or other contracts;

2. Using the network for financial or commercial gain;

3. Degrading or disrupting equipment or system performance;

4. Vandalizing the data of another user;

5. Wastefully using finite resources;

6. Gaining unauthorized access to resources or entities;

7. Invading the privacy of individuals;

8. Using an account owned by another user;

9. Posting personal communications without the author's consent;

10. Posting anonymous messages.

### NuevaNet CONSENT AND WAIVER

By signing the Consent and Waiver form attached, the requestor and his/her parent(s) or guardian(s) (if the requestor is a student) agree to abide by these restrictions. The student and his/her parent(s) or guardian(s) should discuss these rights and responsibilities together.

Further, the requestor and his/her parent(s) or guardian(s) are warned that The Nueva School does not have control of the information on the Internet, nor does it provide any barriers to account holders accessing the full range of information available other than those constraints imposed by finite resources. Other sites accessible via the Internet may contain material that is illegal, defamatory, inaccurate or potentially offensive to some people. While NuevaNet's intent is to make Internet access available to further its educational goals and objectives, account holders will have the ability to access other materials as well.

Nueva believes that the benefits to educators and students from access to the Internet, in the form of information resources and opportunities for collaboration, far exceed any disadvantages of access. But ultimately, parent(s) and guardian(s) of minors are responsible for setting and conveying the standards that their child or ward should follow. To that end, Nueva supports and respects each family's right to decide whether or not to apply for NuevaNet access.

The account holder and, if a minor, his/her parent(s) or guardian(s) must understand that NuevaNet is an experimental system being developed to support Nueva's educational responsibilities and missions. The specific conditions and services being offered will change from time to time. In addition, an account holder uses NuevaNet at his/her own risk. Nueva makes no warranties with respect to NuevaNet service, and it specifically assumes no responsibilities for:

1. The content of any advice or information received by an account holder from a source outside Nueva, or any costs or charges incurred as a result of seeing or accepting such advice;

2. Any costs, liability or damages caused by the way the account holder chooses to use his/her NuevaNet access;

3. Any consequences of service interruptions or changes, even if those disruptions arise from circumstances under the control of Nueva;

4. While NuevaNet supports the privacy of electronic mail, account users must assume that this cannot be guaranteed.

### APPENDICES:

The Nueva Library Selection Policy (revised 2/94)

The Library Bill of Rights of the American Library Association

Interpretations of The Library Bill of Rights

Free Access to Libraries for Minors

Restricted Access to Library Materials

Access to Resources and Services in the School Library Media Program

Access for Children and Young People to Videotapes and Other Nonprint Formats

Statement on Labeling

**Nueva School. NuevaNet Committee. (1993). Acceptable Use Policy. Hillsborough, CA: Nueva School. Available World Wide Web, at**

**http://www.nueva.pvt.k12.ca.us/**

# A Working Document on Copyright and Fair Use for Librarians

This statement was developed by representatives of the following associations:

- American Association of Law Librarians
- American Library Association (the ALA Council approved the statement in principle on February 8, 1995)
- Association of Academic Health Sciences Library Directors
- Association of Research Libraries
- Medical Library Association
- Special Libraries Association

## Fair Use in the Electronic Age: Serving the Public Interest
### *A Working Document from the Library Community*

The following statement is an outgrowth of discussions among a number of library associations regarding intellectual property and, in particular, the concern that the interests and rights of copyright owners and users remain balanced in the digital environment. Its purpose is to outline the lawful uses of copyrighted works by individuals, libraries, and educational institutions in the electronic environment. It is intended to inform ongoing copyright discussions and serve as a reference document for users and libraries, to be circulated widely, and to spark discussion on these issues. The statement will continue to be a Working Document.

### *The Statement*

The genius of United States copyright law is that, in conformance with its constitutional foundation, it balances the intellectual property interests of authors, publishers and copyright owners with society's need for the free exchange of ideas. Taken together, fair use and other public rights to utilize copyrighted works, as confirmed in the Copyright Act of 1976, constitute indispensable legal doctrines for promoting the dissemination of knowledge, while ensuring authors, publishers and copyright owners appropriate protection of their creative works and economic investments.

The fair-use provision of the Copyright Act allows reproduction and other uses of copyrighted works under certain conditions for purposes such as criticism, comment, news reporting, teaching (including multiple copies for classroom use), scholarship, or research. Additional provisions of the law allow uses specifically permitted by Congress to further educational and library activities. The preservation and continuation of these balanced rights in an electronic environment as well as in traditional formats are essential to the free flow of information and to the development of an information infrastructure that serves the public interest.

It follows that the benefits of the new technologies should flow to the public as well as to copyright proprietors. As more information becomes available only in electronic formats, the public's legitimate right to use copyrighted material must be protected. In order for copyright to truly serve its purpose of "promoting progress," the public's right of fair use must continue in the electronic era, and these lawful uses of copyrighted works must be allowed without individual transaction fees.

Without infringing copyright, the public has a right to expect to

- read, listen to, or view publicly marketed copyrighted material privately, on site or remotely;
- browse through publicly marketed copyrighted material;
- experiment with variations of copyrighted material for fair-use purposes, while preserving the integrity of the original;
- make or have made for it a first-generation copy for personal use of an article or other small part of a publicly marketed copyrighted work or a work in a library's collection for such purpose as study, scholarship, or research; and
- make transitory copies if ephemeral or incidental to a lawful use and if retained only temporarily.

Without infringing copyright, nonprofit libraries and other Section 108 libraries, on behalf of their clientele, should be able to

- use electronic technologies to preserve copyrighted materials in their collections;
- provide copyrighted materials as part of electronic reserve room service;
- provide copyrighted materials as part of electronic interlibrary loan service; and
- avoid liability, after posting appropriate copyright notices, for the unsupervised actions of their users.

Users, libraries, and educational institutions have a right to expect that

- the terms of licenses will not restrict fair use or other lawful library or educational uses;
- U.S. government works and other public domain materials will be readily available without restrictions and at a government price not exceeding the marginal cost of dissemination; and
- rights of use for nonprofit education apply in face-to-face teaching and in transmittal or broadcast to remote locations, where educational institutions of the future must increasingly reach their students.

Carefully constructed copyright guidelines and practices have emerged for the print environment to ensure that there is a balance between the rights of users and those of authors, publishers, and copyright owners. New understandings, developed by all stake-holders, will help to ensure that this balance is retained in a rapidly changing electronic environment. This working statement addresses lawful uses of copyrighted works in both the print and electronic environments.

January 18, 1995

# Guidelines for Using and Citing Internet Resources

The burgeoning availability of Internet resources poses a puzzling challenge for educators and researchers: how are such resources properly cited? In a posting to the LM_NET listserv, Drendon (1995) notes, "my experience with citation is that it is too complicated to give a few short rules.... As I wrote elsewhere: 'Citing is such sweet sorrow.' " Information about the citation of electronically stored resources can be found in the newer editions of several style manuals. Unfortunately, such guidance is sketchy and inconsistent.
Li and Crane (1993) wrote a relatively comprehensive guide to electronic information citation, but this earlier treatment of the Internet ignores some of the newer Internet tools. Their revised book (1996) includes both American Psychological Association (APA) and Modern Language Association (MLA) style citations. Presuming (maybe unwisely) to tackle this thorny issue, some suggested guidelines follow.

Citations are meant to credit an author or originator properly for creating a referenced work, and to direct other researchers precisely to the cited source. APA style requires that any cited work include the following elements, in the order listed:

- author(s)
- date
- title, if an article, followed by periodical name
- book title
- medium, if nontraditional (e.g., [on-line])
- volume, number, and paging (some electronic formats defy standard pagination)
- publication location: publisher. Or, electronic service availability: access site (e.g., Available e-mail: LM_NET@listserv.syr.edu)

Users of electronic resources need information about the medium of access (e.g., "on-line" or "CD-ROM"). Researchers are rightfully cautioned to treat punctuation marks very carefully in their citations of on-line sources, lest they be mistaken for parts of an address. By the same token, spaces and capital or lower-case letters should appear exactly as they appear in the electronic address. For more insight into these issues, readers may consult works by Li and Crane, or the fourth edition of the *Publication Manual of the American Psychological Association* (1994).

The Internet is a research tool. Students and teachers should come to view electronic data as perfectly legitimate, and to judge it on the merit of its content, as they would printed information. When using any Internet resource, researchers should treat the results with the respect accorded to traditional sources. Users should therefore:

- honor copyright notices
- honor the intellectual property of other educators by acknowledging sources and maintaining the integrity of original documents
- acknowledge the rare instances when original documents are edited
- teach students about plagiarism and about proper use of information technology. (The tools that make it easy to capture, analyze, and synthesize information electronically also make it easy to plagiarize.)

Media librarians are well aware of these principles. Other users may not be so aware. To help advance the cause of copyright observance and network ethics, chapter 5 offered an in-depth discussion of these issues.

## Citing Resources Found on the World Wide Web

**IN CHAPTER 5,** a document written by Lawrence Magid and available on the Web, was discussed and cited. Fortunately, when a resource is captured on the Web, most browsers present on screen all the information required for a research citation. Magid's piece, *Child Safety on the Information Superhighway*, is available on the Web at the following URL site:

**http://www.4j.lane.edu/**

The pathway to the main directory in which this document can be found is:

**InternetResources/Safety/**

(The forward-slash "/" mark indicates that the identifier immediately to the left is a directory. To the right of the slash will appear a filename or a subdirectory(ies). The filename of the desired file will always be the rightmost identifier. In this case, the filename is:

**Safety.html**

Thus, the citation would appear as follows:

Magid, L. (1994). *Child Safety on the Information Superhighway* [on-line].
  Available WWW: **http://www.4j.lane.edu/**
  Path: **InternetResources/Safety/**
  File: **Safety.html**

Note the use of capital letters and spaces in "InternetResources/Safety/" These are cited exactly as they appear in the document's URL. To cite differently could make it very difficult for another researcher to find this document on the Web.

## Citing and Using Gopher References

**TO CITE A REFERENCE** to a Gopher resource, one needs to provide the host location and any path information needed to navigate from the host's main menu to the actual document or resource. This information is readily available from the Gopher menu. On a

Unix-style Gopher, the user gives the "=" command when the arrow is pointing to the desired resource. On a Windows-style Gopher, the user highlights the desired resource and chooses "Get Attribute Info" from the Gopher pull-down menu. The technical information for the desired resource is given in a box or window on the screen, and it includes the host and path for the particular resource. For example, a lesson plan for creative thinking found on the AskERIC Gopher has the following attributes in TurboGopher:

```
+INFO: 1Miscellaneous 1/Lesson/Miscellaneous ericir.syr.edu 70 +
+ADMIN:
Admin: Nancy Morgan or R. David Lankes +1 (315)443-3640
<nmorgan@ericir.syr.edu or rdlankes@ericir.syr.edu>
Mod-Date: Fri Feb 4 12:42:15 1994 <19940204124215>
TTL: 180
+VIEWS:
application/gopher-menu En-US: <2k>
application/gopher+-menu En-US: <2k>
text/html En_US: <2k>
```

The important information in this example is contained in the first line of the entry. The *hostname* is

### ericir.syr.edu

(70 is the standard port number for Gopher servers), and the *pathname* from the top-level menu (1) is

### /Lesson/Miscellaneous

This means that the user would choose "Lesson..." from the main menu at this Gopher site and then choose "Miscellaneous. . ." from the "Lesson . . ." submenu.

The hostname and pathname information are as vital as publisher and place of publication for conventional references, but they tend to change, making them hard for future users to track down. The lesson plan mentioned earlier was authored by Linda Huff, and it would be cited as follows:

Huff, L. (1994). *Apples* [on-line].
Available Gopher: **Gopher://ericir.syr.edu/**
Path: **Lesson/Miscellaneous**

# Citing References to E-mail and Newsgroups

**PERSONAL E-MAIL MESSAGES** should be cited in the following way: the "author" is the original sender of a message. The "date" is the date on which the message was first sent. Determining that date may require the user to read through the message header, as many messages are forwarded several times before reaching the user. The "title" is the subject line of the message. After the title, indicate that the reference is to an Internet e-mail message, followed by the recipient's e-mail address. The following e-mail message carried the header (abridged for simplicity) as shown here:

```
Received: from umassd.edu by umassd.edu (PMDF
V4.2-15 #3948) id
<01HU5PFWXW2O8Y595G@umassd.edu>; Wed, 16 Aug
1995 23:12:48 EDT

Date: Wed, 16 Aug 1995 23:12:48 -0400 (EDT)
From: JKAPUT@umassd.edu
Subject: DDP Benchmarks from John LeBaron
To: lebaronj@woods.uml.edu, rlesh@nsf.gov
Message-ID: <01HU5PFWY5PU8Y595G@umassd.edu>
Organization: University of Massachusetts
Dartmouth, North Dartmouth, MA
X-VMS-To: IN:: "lebaronj@woods.uml.edu"
X-VMS-Cc: JKAPUT
```

This message from Dr. James Kaput was sent on August 16, 1995. It would be cited as:

> Kaput, J. (1995, August 16). *DDP benchmarks from John LeBaron* [e-mail to J. LeBaron] [on-line].
> Available e-mail: **lebaronj@woods.uml.edu**

Aside from contacting the sender or the person citing the message, there is normally no way for the reader of the citation to locate and retrieve a copy of a personal message. Listserv messages are cited somewhat differently, as illustrated in the helpful guideline sent to the LM_NET listserv on July 25, 1995, by Katie Bailey of the Seabreeze High School in Daytona Beach, Florida. The abbreviated message header for her listserv contribution was:

```
Received: from listserv.syr.edu
(listserv@listserv.syr.edu [128.230.1.252])
Date: Tue, 25 Jul 1995 15:11:24 (EST)

From: Katie Bailey <BAILEYK@MAIL.FIRN.EDU>
Subject: Re: Citing Internet Sources
To: Multiple recipients of list LM_NET
<LM_NET@LISTSERV.SYR.EDU>
```

Katie's message would be cited this way:

> Bailey, K. (1995, July 25). *Re: citing Internet sources* [LM_NET listserv] [on-line].
> Available e-mail: **LM_NET@listserv.syr.edu**

Tracking down this distributed message is relatively easy, because the LM_NET listserv is archived at the ERIC Web and Gopher servers at Syracuse University.

Now, let us assume the plausible scenario that Dr. Kaput's e-mail message to John LeBaron had been posted publicly on the same date to the "bit.listserv.edtech" newsgroup. As with e-mail, the message header will provide the information needed for a citation. The citation would closely resemble the e-mail citation, and appear as:

> Kaput, J. (1995, August 16). *DDP benchmarks from John LeBaron* [newsgroup posting] [on-line].
> Available Newsgroups: **bit.listserv.edtech**

# Telnet Citations and Use

**A TELNET SESSION** to a remote computer will produce a rather large variety of "entry" screens and procedures. Therefore, users need to keep track of their pathways to research files to cite them properly. Sometimes, Telnet sessions will bring a user to a Gopher server on the remote computer. Some Internet sites may not offer Gopher clients, so the Telnet pathway to a desired resource may be essential.

As an example, the document *Opportunities for Future Development in Energy Education for Environmental Stewardship* (1994) is available in the UMassK12 Gopher server, which may be accessed by Telnetting to **k12.ucs.umass.edu** After one logs in as a "guest," a "GUEST MENU" screen appears. On this screen, Item 10 offers the UMassK12 Gopher. On the Gopher menu, Item 1 is the "4-H Energy Education Resource Database/" When this directory is opened, Item 9 presents "Report to 4-H" Selecting this item brings up this document, produced by the UMass Cooperative Extension System. The citation for this file would be:

> University of Massachusetts Cooperative Extension System. (1994). *Opportunities for Future Development in Energy Education for Environmental Stewardship* [on-line].
> Available Telnet: **k12.ucs.umass.edu/**
> Path: **GUEST MENU/UMassK12 Gopher/4-H Energy Education Resource Database/**
> File: **Report to 4-H**

# Citing and Using FTP Sources

**USERS WILL FIND REFERENCES** to FTP files in two formats, the "old-fashioned way," and the newer, usually preferred URL format. To retrieve the file called *An Incomplete Guide to the Internet and Other Telecommunications Opportunities Especially for Teachers and Students K-12* (referenced later), users would open an FTP connection to the indicated host. They would then log in as "anonymous" and give their full Internet address as the password. After connecting to the correct directory ("cd *pathname*"), they would transfer the file ("get *filename*") and then exit FTP. In this example, the session would appear as follows on the user's VAX/VMS host, where the user's response is shown in a computer screen font:

```
$ FTP
FTP> open ftp.ncsa.uiuc.edu <return>
username: anonymous <return>
password: collierc@woods.uml.edu <return>
cd Education/Education_Resources <return>
get Incomplete_Guide <return>
close <return>
FTP exit <return>
```

The "traditional" FTP citation to NCSA's guide to Internet use in schools would appear as follows:

> NCSA Education Group. (1993). *An incomplete guide to the Internet: and other telecommunications opportunities especially for teachers and students k-12* [on-line].

Available FTP: **ncsa.uiuc.edu/**
Path: **Education/Education_Resources/**
File: **Incomplete_Guide**

If this same file were downloaded via the World Wide Web, as it can be, the citation would include the URL format of the FTP host, the directory path, and the filename:

**FTP://hostname/pathname(s)/filename**

For example, the Web-accessed citation for the *Incomplete Guide* would be:

NCSA Education Group. (1993). *An incomplete guide to the Internet: and other telecommunications opportunities especially for teachers and students k-12* [on-line].
Available WWW: **FTP://ftp.ncsa.uiuc.edu/**
Path: **Education/Education_Resources/**
File: **Incomplete_Guide**

# Citations: Rich Information Sources

**TODAY MANY SITES OFFER ASSISTANCE** in citing information obtained from on-line sources. When the first draft of this book was completed in October, 1995, though, there were only a few sites in existence. By April, 1996, a profusion of helper sites had appeared. These sites now include:

Hawaii Education and Research Network (Cyber Citations)
**http://www.hern.hawaii.edu/hern/resources/misc_sites.html**

Chico High School Research and Writing Tips
**http://www.chs.chico.k12.ca.us/libr/webres/res.html**

MLA-Style Citations of Electronic Sources by Janice R. Walker
**http://www.cas.usf.edu/english/walker/mla.html**

Web Extension to APA Style
**http://www.nyu.edu/pages/psychology/WEAPAS/**

APA Publication Manual Crib Sheet
**http://www.gasou.edu/psychweb/tipsheet/apacrib.htm**

Citation Formats
**http://www.cc.emory.edu/WHSCL/citation.formats.html**

APA Style Guide
**http://www.pitt.edu/~grouprev/Language/apa-cite-forms/**

Citations of Electronic Documents in an Electronic Document by Haines Brown
**http://neal.ctstateu.edu/history/cite.html**

Bibliographic Formats for Citing Electronic Information
**http://www.uvm.edu/~xli/reference/estyles.html**

A Brief Citation Guide for Internet Sources in History and the Humanities by Melvin E. Page
**Gopher://h-net.msu.edu:70/00/lists/H-AFRICA/internet-cit/**

Guide for Citing Electronic Information (William Paterson College)
**http://www.wilpaterson.edu/wpcpages/library/citing.htm**

Another site that is useful when researching and writing is:

**http://www.columbia.edu/acis/bartleby/strunk/**

This site does not contain information on citing electronic sources, but does contain the original version of Strunk's *The Elements of Style* (1918), an invaluable writing guide.

# References

American Psychological Association. 1994. *Publication manual of the American Psychological Association.* 4th ed. Washington, D.C.: American Psychological Association.

Brendon, L. 1995, September 8. *HIT: Citing WWW and Internet Info.* [LM_NET listserv] [on-line]. Available e-mail: **LM_NET@listserv.syr.edu**

Li, X., and N. B. Crane. 1993. *Electronic style: A guide to citing electronic information.* Westport, Conn.: Meckler.

———. 1996. *Electronic style: A guide to citing electronic information.* Rev. ed. Westport, Conn.: Mecklermedia.

Strunk, W., Jr. 1918. *The elements of style.* Geneva, N.Y.: Press of W. P. Humphrey.

Strunk, W., Jr., and E. B. White. 1959. *The elements of style.* New York: Macmillan.

# Resources for Further Reading

*Chicago Manual of Style.* 14th ed. Chicago: University of Chicago Press, 1993.

"Citing Internet resources: How students should reference online sources in their bibliographies." *Classroom Connect* 2, no. 6 (1996): 9.

Gibaldi, J. *MLA Handbook for Writers of Research Papers.* 4th ed. New York: Modern Language Association of America, 1995.

Turabian, K. L. *A Manual for Writers of Term Papers, Theses, and Dissertations.* 5th ed. Chicago: University of Chicago Press, 1987.

**acceptable use policy (AUP).**  Written rules and responsibilities, usually published by a network operator, that establish the conditions under which users may access network services. Breaches of an AUP may result in the termination of user privileges.

**Advanced Research Projects Agency (ARPA).**  An agency of the United States Department of Defense. As the Internet's original ancestor, ARPAnet was created as a robust computer network designed to carry critical data in times of military emergency.

**alias.**  A substitute term or "nickname" created in a computer system as a pointer to some other application, file, directory, or data set. Alphabetized Internet addresses are aliases for an underlying nomenclature of numbers and dots.

**AltaVista.**  See *search engine.*

**American Standard Code for Information Interchange (ASCII).**  A standard system of computer codes to represent text characters on the keyboard. ASCII is common to all operating platforms. It is limited to pure text, and is unable to interpret any other kind of data (graphic, sound, audio).

**analog signal.**  An electronic signal (such as a television signal) produced and transmitted according to a continually varying waveform. Conventional television generates analog signals because current broadcast procedures require analog signals for full-motion production and transmission.

**applet.**  A software application designed to enhance the capability of creating or reading WWW files with a GUI browser.

**Archie.**  See *search engine.*

**ARPA.**  See *Advanced Research Projects Agency.*

**ASCII.**  See *American Standard Code for Information Interchange.*

**AskERIC.**  A service for educators provided on the Internet by the ERIC Clearinghouse at Syracuse University. Resources include question answering, search of the ERIC database, collection of lesson plans, full text of ERIC digests, and InfoGuides to Internet resources for education.

**asynchronous communication.**  Electronic communication characterized by a time delay between the posting and the receipt of information. The opposite of this is *synchronous communication,* where two or more parties are communicating simultaneously and interactively; that is, in *real time.*

**AUP.**  See *acceptable use policy.*

**backbone.**  The primary, highest level infrastructure of an electronic network, where secondary network systems feed in and out. In a state, for example, K–12 school LANs might feed into (and take from) a state-operated backbone.

**bandwidth.**  The difference between the highest and lowest frequencies that a system can transmit. Higher bandwidths can carry more information than lower bandwidths.

**BBS.**  See *bulletin board system.*

**biometric device.** A form of network security that allows access according to a user's unique biological attributes, such as voice pattern or fingerprint.

**BITNET (Because It's Time Network).** A wide area network of academic and r esearch computers. In many locations, BITNET membership has been superseded by institutional affiliation with the Internet.

**bits per second (bps).** A rate at which digitized signals are transferred from one data-manipulating device (for example, a computer) to another. For example, a 14,400-bps modem is capable of sending and receiving 14,400 bits per second to and from a connected computer.

**blocking software.** Software that electronically screens out network-supplied material deemed offensive, indecent, or obscene. Through the use of such software, targeted material will not appear on the user's client desktop computer.

**bookmark.** A feature in Gopher and the WWW browsers that allows users to "mark" frequently visited locations so that they may revisit without searching for or re-entering the identifying address.

**Boolean operator.** The logical functions "AND," "OR," and "NOT," used as part of a keyword search strategy that allows users to define and limit the scope of their searches. Searches that use these operators between keywords tend to produce a relevant and manageable list of hits. (See *hit*.)

**bps.** See *bits per second*.

**browser.** Computer network interface software that enables navigation (or browsing) of a particular network tool. See *World Wide Web*.

**bulletin board system (BBS).** A computer-networked electronic clearinghouse where account holders may post public notices in much the same manner as paper notices are posted on a conventional bulletin board. Some BBS systems are local in scope. USENET newsgroups are very broad-based BBS systems.

**button.** See *hot spot*.

**channel service unit (CSU).** Sometimes called "customer service unit." An interface between a telephone terminal and a data terminal that regenerates a transmitted signal and checks for transmission errors.

**chat.** Computer network tools that allow real-time exchanges of information between and among remotely located network users. An example is Internet Relay Chat.

**client.** See *client-server*.

**client-server.** A model of distributed networking in which a "server" computer provides resources and file storage space for "client" computers to use interactively. Client programs interact with the user (for example, allowing the user to read, compose, and address e-mail messages), while the server programs operate in the background on behalf of multiple clients (for example, to store and forward messages for a LAN and to send and receive mail via the Internet).

**coaxial cable.** Shielded metal cable capable of carrying large quantities of data, including full-motion video, over relatively long distances. Typically used for television signal transmission by commercial cable television operations. Also capable of carrying voice, image, and data signals.

**codec (CODer/DEcoder).** A device that converts analog audio and video signals into digital form, compressing the data for transmission and then reversing the process at the receiving end.

**connectivity.** The capacity of different computer systems to function interactively between networks. The connectivity between some networks may be limited to e-mail exchange; others may allow a fuller range of interoperability that permits file sharing, hypermedia browsing, and remote logins.

**CSU.** See *channel service unit.*

**CU-SeeMe.** A popular, public domain videoconferencing tool for the Internet, developed at Cornell University. See *teleconference.*

**desktop videoconference.** Videoconference in which the technology is provided by desktop computers linked by a network and equipped with cameras, microphones, and speakers.

**dial-up connection.** Slower speed connection through a dial-up modem (typically ranging between 1,200 bps and 56 kbps). Traditionally, dial-up connections support a terminal-host connection, but newer arrangements and accounts support client-server interactions through PPP or SLIP with 4.4 kpbs or faster connections.

**digital signal.** An electronic signal that is transmitted in binary digits to reduce the effect of errors introduced by signal noise.

**direct internet connection.** A high-bandwidth connection (usually 56 kbps or higher) that allows a computer to participate fully on the Internet as a client or server or both (in contrast to the computer acting as a dumb terminal connected to an Internet host)

**distributed network.** See *client-server.*

**domain name.** The unique name assigned to each of the Internet's member computers or computer systems. The domain name allows each member node to be accurately addressed by users from remote locations.

**download.** To copy onto a local computer files or data from a remote computer or computer system.

**dumb terminal.** See *terminal host.*

**e-mail (electronic mail).** Messages (typically private) composed on computers and directed to other computer-resident electronic addresses.

**electronic mail.** See *e-mail.*

**electronic whiteboard.** The common workspace between two or more networked computers where multiple users may simultaneously work on the same files.

**encryption.** Coding procedure that bars remote access to confidential networked material, or that bars access by certain classes of users to networked materials deemed inappropriate.

**Ethernet.** A commonly installed kind of local area network that supports very fast data transmission speeds (typically 10 million bits per second). Many networked computers that run TCP/IP are connected to the Internet through an Ethernet LAN.

**FAQs.** See *frequently asked questions.*

**fiber optic.** A relatively new kind of "cable" capable of transmitting video, voice, and data signals over long distances. Signals are transmitted as light pulses through microscopically thin strands of flexible glass.

**file server.** A computer that provides access to applications and files for other desktop computers in a local area network. A file server may have a larger disk storage capacity than the client computers it serves.

**File Transfer Protocol (FTP).** A standard procedure that allows files to be transferred between networked computer systems. The need to transfer files accurately was one of the driving motivations behind the original creation of the Internet.

**Finger.** An Internet tool through which information about account holders on certain other Internet member systems may be found.

**firewall.** A network security mechanism that allows a local node access to an external network while prohibiting outside access to the local node.

**flame.** An angry, confrontational, or derogatory personal message sent over a computer network, often on an e-mail listserv or a bulletin board system.

**freenet.** A community information server that provides network resources, services, and Internet access via ordinary telephone lines.

**freeware.** See *public domain software.*

**frequently asked questions (FAQs).** A standard list of questions and answers posted publicly by many Internet service providers about access to and use of their resources.

**FTP.** See *File Transfer Protocol.*

**gateway.** A device that connects computer networks that use different communications protocols (e.g., Ethernet and Token Ring). It performs the translation among protocols, permitting them to communicate properly.

**GIF.** See *Graphic Interchange Format.*

**gigabyte.** One billion bytes of data. Used in reference to the storage or transmission of massive amounts of information.

**Gopher.** A searchable Internet network application, originally developed at the University of Minnesota, that serves menus of information to network clients. Gopher servers around the world are linked in a manner that allows any client to access any active server at any time. The global aggregation of Gopher data is called GopherSpace.

**GopherSpace.** See *Gopher.*

**Graphic Interchange Format (GIF).** A file format that enables the creation and use of high-quality graphic images within and across networks.

**graphical user interface (GUI).** A computer application program or utility that allows the user to interact through icons, buttons, hot spots, menus, or other graphical objects, rather than by typing in a command line. Netscape is an example of a GUI Web browser, whereas Lynx is a command-line browser.

**GUI (pronounced "gooey").** See *graphical user interface.*

**handshake.** The "negotiation" process by which two computers come to agree on a common communication protocol when establishing a network connection.

**hard wire.** An electronic pathway connecting two or more telecommunicating devices made possible by physical wiring.

**helper applications.** Software that understands and displays a particular graphical format, such as Sparkle for MPEG video or Sound Machine for "aiff" audio files. See *applet.*

**hit.** A listed item or a resource produced by an interactive database search.

**home page.** The local starting point for a hypermedia resource on the World Wide Web. Analogous to a home card in a HyperCard, Toolbox, or other hypermedia stack.

**hot spot.** Screen display that appears on a World Wide Web browser or a hypermedia application window as highlighted or colored text, an icon, a button, or another object linked to further information anywhere on the Web.

**host.** The "home" computer or computer system that serves remotely connected users.

**HTML.** See *HyperText Markup Language.*

**hub.** A regional computer server that ties local member users into a larger wide area network.

**hybrid telecommunications system.** A communications network constructed from a combination of different technologies for signal transmission and receipt.

**hypermedia.** A form of multimedia (combined sound, image, text, graphics, and video) that is interactive or navigable. That is, the user can choose designated hot spots that link to information of interest, rather than having to follow a linear or sequential presentation of information.

**hypertext.** Displayed text on a computer screen that provides direct, interactive links or pathways to other related resources when activated by pointing and clicking with a mouse or by some other command. Web browsers display hypertext as hot spots that facilitate browsing on the World Wide Web.

**HyperText Markup Language (HTML).** The conventional format for describing a home page or any of its links. HTML is interpreted by a Web browser, such as Lynx or Netscape, when the browser presents a home page to the user's screen.

**icon.** A computer screen image that launches a computer operation by user command. Such commands are typically executed by pointing at the icon with a mouse and clicking on it.

**I-loop (institutional loop).** Selected channels of a cable television service in a municipality that are reserved for use by municipal institutions.

**ILS.** See *integrated learning system.*

**I-net (institutional network).** Normally, two channels of the I-Loop that are used for data communication. Transmission of data on cable television channels requires data communication equipment at each building to convert signals to the building's local area network.

**information superhighway.** See *National Information Infrastructure.*

**InfoSeek.** See *search engine.*

**infrastructure.** The system of electronic pathways by which a computer is interconnected with other computers through local, regional, national, and global networks. The national highway system of interstate and state highways, secondary roads, and city streets is a transportation infrastructure. The various networks that make up the Internet constitute an information infrastructure.

**institutional loop.** See *I-loop.*

**institutional network.** See *I-net.*

**integrated learning system (ILS).** An integrated and centralized network of computer hardware and instructional software. Workstation sites typically function as client nodes on a server that provides a full menu of prepackaged software ranging from curricular content to teacher management tools for record-keeping, grading, and other instruction-related administrative tasks.

**Integrated Services Digital Network (ISDN).** A telecommunication service provided by several telephone companies in the United States and abroad. Because this service offers a relatively high bandwidth, it is being promoted as an integrated "catch-all" capable of transmitting a full range of voice, data, and visual information.

**Internet Service Provider (ISP).** A commercial service that provides Internet access to subscribers for a fee. Such service is available in many areas and Internet access is now being sold by an increasing number of traditional telephone companies.

**internetwork.** Many different computer networks operating on a variety of platforms but able to function as parts of a systemic whole. The Internet is an example of internetworking, but it is not a network as such.

**IP (Internet Protocol).** See Transmission Control Protocol/Internet Protocol.

**ISDN.** See Integrated Services Digital Network.

**ISP.** See Internet Service Provider.

**kbps.** See *kilobits per second.*

**keyword.** A word or term contained within a database or directory of databases on which user searches may "key." A keyword search will locate and list records containing the desired word.

**kilobits per second (kbps).** A measurement of data transmission speed in thousands of bits per second, usually in reference to a wide area network or dial-up connection to a remote computer.

**LAN.** See *local area network.*

**listserv.** A distributed e-mail membership list, often provided on the Internet by special interest groups or professional associations. All members of a listserv may post messages to, or receive messages from, other members of the list. "Listproc," "majordomo," and "mailserv" are other e-mail distribution systems.

**local area network (LAN).** Cabling and other equipment, such as bridges and interface cards, within a building or several buildings that support high-speed transmission of data among computers. Examples are 1 mbps ThinNet, 10 mbps Ethernet, and 10 mbps Token Ring systems.

**login (logon, logoff, logout).** Entering (login or logon) or exiting (logoff or logout) a host computer system via modem or some other means of network connection.

**Lycos.** See *search engine.*

**Lynx.** A telecommunication software browser that enables text-driven navigation of the World Wide Web.

**majordomo.** See *listserv.*

**mbps.** See *megabits per second.*

**megabits per second (mbps).** A measurement of transmission speed, usually in reference to a local area network, which operates at 1 to 10 million bits per second or higher.

**meta search engine.** A search engine of search engines that simultaneously scans several smaller engines in response to a single request. MetaCrawler and Savvy are examples.

**Microsoft Internet Explorer.** Telecommunication software browser that allows icon-driven navigation of the World Wide Web.

**microwave.** A high-frequency wave capable of carrying data, television, and radio signals, usually for relatively short distances. Microwave signals can be transmitted from an origination antenna to another single point, or can be diffused from an origination point to several reception sites at once.

**mirror site.** A second-tier network node that arranges with a home FTP site to carry and make available certain publicly accessible files. Mirror sites help to alleviate Internet traffic for popular files that are in great demand.

**modem (MOdulator/DEModulator).** A device that connects remotely located computers. It converts the digital computer signals into analog signals that can be transmitted over telephone lines, while simultaneously converting analog data to digital signals that can be read by a computer.

**MOSAIC.** Telecommunication software browser that enables icon-driven navigation of the World Wide Web.

**multimedia.** A combination of text, image, sound, and/or any other communication medium in a computer-driven operation. Computer driven devices such as CD-ROM players often enable multimedia computer operations, as do advanced, high-capacity Internet interfaces such as Netscape and Microsoft Internet Explorer.

**multiplexer.** A device used to transmit signals from several different sources over a single channel.

**National Information Infrastructure (NII).** A national telecommunication capacity project of many government and private sector organizations designed to carry very high volumes of data at exceedingly high speeds. The NII is intended to cover a multitude of public and private purposes, and to serve all geographic areas and demographic needs equitably.

**netiquette.** Standards of courtesy and consideration to which computer network users are expected to adhere. Some of these conventions can be found in written form; others make up a growing unwritten code of commonly accepted practice in the network community.

**Netscape.** Telecommunication software browser that enables icon-driven navigation of the World Wide Web.

**network.** An interconnected community of electronic communication devices, such as computers, through which various kinds of information may be shared. Newer computer networks are interactive, enabling any connected device to both originate and receive information. More traditional networks, such as broadcast television, only allow one-way communication from a single source to multiple recipients.

**newsgroup.** A public, networked discussion forum for individuals interested in particular topics. As distinct from e-mail listservs, newsgroup users may read, post, reply to, and follow up on newsgroup messages without their own personal subscriptions. Access to a newsgroup requires news reader interface software.

**NII.** See *National Information Infrastructure.*

**node.** An Internet member computer or networked computer system. Each individual Internet member possesses its own unique domain name and Internet Protocol (IP) number.

**on-line.** When the computer is actually connected by a modem or other telecommunication device to another computer on a network.

**operating system.** See *platform.*

**partial T1.** A meaningful fraction (often one-quarter or a multiple thereof) of a T1 line that can be made available to a customer who does not want or need full T1 capacity.

**platform.** A computer operating system; often incompatible with other kinds of operating system. For example, DOS, Macintosh, and Windows represent unique operating platforms.

**plug-in.** A software application configured with a WWW GUI browser that enables access to certain kinds of files (e.g., files with audio or motion pictures) that the browser cannot reach on its own. See *applet.*

**Point-to-Point Protocol (PPP).** A telecommunications protocol that allows standard telephone lines to be used for full, graphic navigation of the Internet. PPP connections require higher speed modems of 14.4 kbps or faster.

**PPP.** See *Point-to-Point Protocol.*

**protocol.** A "language" that governs the format of network communication, enabling networked computers to function in harmony. TCP/IP is the protocol that allows Internet computers to communicate interactively in a common system.

**public domain software.** Computer software that is made available to users entirely free of charge. Much public domain software is available for downloading from sites on the Internet.

**real time.** In contrast to asynchronous communication, such as electronic mail or voice mail, real-time communication is characterized by simultaneous participation by all parties, such as in a telephone conversation or live videoconference.

**reflector site.** A network server that allows the simultaneous connection of several different interconnected voice, image, and/or data transmissions to occur simultaneously in a real-time teleconference.

**router.** A networked computer or similar device that stores network addresses and determines the path for routing information to and from the computers in a network.

**search engine.** Database query software that executes searches in response to specific user commands. These commands are sometimes expressed as keyword entries, and they launch searches for words contained in files or file directories. For example, Veronica is used for Gopher searches; Alta Vista is used in World Wide Web browsing; Archie is used to locate remote files at public FTP sites.

**Serial Line Internet Protocol (SLIP).** See *Point-to-Point Protocol.*

**server.** See *client-server.*

**shareware.** Computer software that is made available to users at no initial ("up-front") cost. If the software is adopted by the user, however, payment is expected according to conditions stipulated by the producer or the distributor. Much shareware is available for downloading on the Internet.

**SLIP (Serial Line Internet Protocol).** See *Point-to-Point Protocol.*

**snail mail.** A term used by computer network mavens to denote conventional mail operated by national postal services.

**spamming.** The practice of using free public network facilities for commercial advertising or promotion. Though considered an uncommon delicacy among epicures, spam is not regarded as netiquette-correct.

**Switched-56.** A moderately high-capacity leased telephone service available from regional and long-distance telephone companies to support the transmission of large amounts of digital data (voice, computer, video). Server-supported local area computer networks may require Switched-56 service for adequate, collective access to external, global, wide area networks such as the Internet.

**synchronous communication.** See *asynchronous communication.*

**sysop (SYStem OPerator).** An individual responsible for coordinating and moderating account holder message traffic on an electronic bulletin board or conference system.

**T1.** A high-capacity telephone transmission line capable of carrying 1.544 megabits per second of data (equivalent to 24 channels of ordinary telephone signals).

**T3.** An ultrahigh-capacity telephone transmission line capable of carrying roughly 45 megabits per second of data (approximately 30 channels of T-1 grade signals, or 700 channels of ordinary telephone signals).

**TCP/IP.** See *Transmission Control Protocol/Internet Protocol.*

**teleconference.** The simultaneous transmission of images and/or other data that allows individuals at two or more remote locations to carry on a conference or a meeting. Teleconferences typically carry video images so that participants may see each other while they talk. A simple telephone conversation is a basic form of teleconference.

**Telnet.** An Internet tool that allows users to log in remotely from their own computers to other Internet member computers.

**terminal.** See *terminal-host.*

**terminal-host.** A model of networking in which a large "host" computer does the computing while users interact through a "dumb" devices called terminals. The terminals allow interaction through keyboards but have no additional desktop intelligence, such as the applications and tools found in today's personal computers.

**Transmission Control Protocol/Internet Protocol (TCP/IP).** The common system of operations and commands that enables Internet computers to function interactively and systematically. Individual member computers operate locally on a variety of operating platforms (e.g., DOS, Windows, Unix, Macintosh). Internet operations are common to all and conform to the TCP/IP protocol.

**Uniform Resource Locator (URL).** The network address convention used for various Internet tools accessed via the World Wide Web. URL addresses are formatted as protocol:// followed by a code for the host institution identified by the URL.

**Unix.** A computer operating system characterized by a menu/command style interface.

**Unix-style.** An applications interface driven by commands typed in response to screen menus. Unix-style interfaces cannot be driven by the mouse-activated pointing-and-clicking that GUI interfaces make possible.

**upload.** To use a local computer to transmit files to one or more remote computers or computer systems.

**URL.** See *Uniform Resource Locator.*

**USENET.** A loose coalition of networked computer users who constitute the membership of the thousands of Internet-accessible newsgroups.

**user name.** The unique name assigned to an account holder in a computer network. This name usually forms the leftmost identifier in an e-mail address.

**Veronica.** See *search engine.*

**videoconference.** See *teleconference.*

**virus.** A code, maliciously embedded within a computer program, that, when executed, endlessly replicates itself, destroying previously uninfected files throughout a storage medium.

**WAIS.** See *Wide Area Information Server.*

**WAN.** See *wide area network.*

**Web.** See *World Wide Web.*

**WebCrawler.** See *search engine.*

**Wide Area Information Server (WAIS).** An Internet data searching protocol that enables searching of a wide range of Internet-accessible data. WAIS is not limited to any particular Internet tool; thus, the scope of its searches is extremely broad.

**wide area network (WAN).** A system of networked computers with a broader reach than a single building or institution. This reach can range from local to global.

**window.** The portion of a computer screen that represents a particular application, file, folder, directory, or active telecommunications session, as distinct from the remainder of the screen.

**wireless communication.** The interconnection of electronic communication devices without the use of physical wires or cables. Wireless communications use radio signals of various bandwidth frequencies.

**World Wide Web (the Web or WWW).** A global aggregation of data that can be accessed from a vast array of linked resources simply by choosing highlighted words or icons on the home page or root file of a browser such as Netscape (a hypermedia version) or Lynx (a text-only version).

**worm.** An electronic viral infection that operates on and damages whole networks. See *virus*.

**WWW.** See *World Wide Web*.

**Yahoo.** See *search engine*.

American Association of School Librarians. *ICONnect: How to connect to the Internet.* Chicago: American Library Association, 1996.

Barth, R. *Improving schools from within: Teachers, parents, and principals can make a difference.* San Francisco: Jossey-Bass, 1991.

Beane, J. "The middle school: The natural home of integrated curriculum." *Educational Leadership* 49, no. 2 (1991): 9–13.

Benson, A. C. *The complete Internet companion for librarians.* New York: Neal-Schuman, 1995.

Blanchard, K., and S. Johnson. *The one-minute manager.* New York: Berkeley Books, 1981.

Bloom, B. S. *Taxonomy of educational objectives: Cognitive domain* New York: McKay, 1956.

Boe, T., C. Graubart, and M. Cappo. *World desk: A student handbook to Gopher and the World-Wide Web.* Santa Cruz, Calif.: Learning in Motion, 1995.

Brandt, R. "On interdisciplinary curriculum: A conversation with Heidi Hays Jacobs." *Educational Leadership* 49, no. 2 (1991): 24–26.

Bruner, J. S. *The process of education.* Cambridge, Mass.: Harvard University Press, 1961.

Butler, M. *How to use the Internet.* Emeryville, Calif.: Ziff-Davis, 1994.

Calhoun, E. *How to use action-research in the self-renewing school.* Alexandria, Va.: Association for Supervision and Curriculum Development, 1994.

Carlson, R. 1993. *Developing supplemental funding: Initiatives for rural and small schools.* ERIC Digest. March; EDRS No. 357 910.

Cheswick, W. R., and S. M. Bellovin. *Firewalls and Internet security: Repelling the wily hacker.* Reading, Mass.: Addison-Wesley, 1994.

*Classroom Connect.* Wentworth Worldwide Media, Inc. 1866 Colonial Village Drive, P.O. Box 10488, Lancaster, PA 17601-6704. Published nine times a year. To subscribe, e-mail to: **connect@wentworth.com**
For additional information: **http://www.classroom.net/**

Deal, T. E. "Reframing reform." *Educational Leadership* 47, no. 8 (1990): 6–12.

Dern, D. P. *The Internet guide for new users.* New York: McGraw-Hill, 1994.

Descy, D. "Create your own home page: A step-by-step guide." *Technology Connection* 3, no. 2 (1996): 19–21.

Dewey, J. *Democracy and education.* New York: Macmillan, 1916.

———. *Experience and education.* New York: Macmillan, 1938.

Doll, R. C. *Curriculum improvement.* 9th ed. Boston: Allyn & Bacon, 1995.

Drake, S. *Planning integrated curriculum: The call to adventure.* Alexandria, Va.: Association for Supervision and Curriculum Development, 1993.

Drake, S. M. "How our team dissolved the boundaries." *Educational Leadership* 49, no. 2 (1991): 20–22.

Eisenberg, M. "Curriculum mapping and implementation of an elementary school library media skills curriculum." *School Library Media Quarterly* 12, no. 2 (1984): 411–18.

Eisenberg, M. B., and R. E. Berkowitz. *Curriculum initiative: An agenda and strategy for library media programs.* Norwood, N.J.: Ablex, 1988.

Eisner, E. W. *The educational imagination.* New York: Macmillan, 1985.

*Electronic Learning.* Scholastic, Inc. 2931 East McCarty Street, P.O. Box 3710, Jefferson City, MO 65102-3710. Published six times a year. For additional information: **http://www.scholastic.com/public/EL/EL.html**

Frazier, D. "Envision the future: Ask a student." *MultiMedia Schools* 2, no. 5 (1995): 44–46.

Frazier, G. G., and D. Frazier. *Telecommunications and education: Surfing and the art of change.* Alexandria, Va.: National School Boards Technology Leadership Network, 1994.

Gagné, R. M. *The conditions of learning.* New York: Holt, Rinehart & Winston, 1965.

Goldberg, B., and J. Richards. "Leveraging technology for reform: Changing schools and communities into learning organizations." *Educational Technology* 35, no. 5 (1995): 5–16.

Good, T., and J. E. Brophy. *Looking in classrooms.* New York: Harper & Row, 1984.

Goodlad, J. I. *A place called school: Prospects for the future.* New York: McGraw-Hill, 1984.

Hahn, H., and R. Strut. *The Internet complete reference.* Berkeley, Calif.: Osborne McGraw-Hill, 1994.

Harmon, C., ed. *Using the Internet, online services, and CD-ROMs for writing research and term papers.* New York: Neal-Schuman, 1995.

Harmon, C., and A. K. Symons. *Protecting the right to read: A how-to-do-it manual for school and public librarians.* New York: Neal-Schuman, 1995.

Harris, J. *Way of the ferret: Finding and using educational resources on the Internet.* 2d ed. Eugene, Oreg.: International Society for Technology in Education, 1995.

Illich, I. *Deschooling society.* New York: Harper & Row, 1970.

Jackson, P. *Life in classrooms.* New York: Holt, Rinehart & Winston, 1968.

Jacobs, H. H. "Planning for curriculum integration." *Educational Leadership* 49, no. 2 (1991): 27–28.

Jacobs, H. H., ed. *Interdisciplinary curriculum: Design and implementation.* Alexandria, Va.: Association for Supervision and Curriculum Development, 1989.

Joyce, B., ed. *Changing school culture through staff development* (1990 Yearbook of the Association for Supervision and Curriculum Development). Alexandria, Va.: Association for Supervision and Curriculum Development, 1990.

Joyce, B., J. Wolf, and E. Calhoun. *The self-renewing school.* Alexandria, Va.: Association for Supervision and Curriculum Development, 1993.

Kozol, Jonathan. *Savage inequalities: Children in America's schools.* New York: Crown, 1991.

Kuhlthau, C. C., M. E. Goodin, and M. J. McNally, eds. *Assessment and the school library media center.* Englewood, Colo.: Libraries Unlimited, 1994.

Kurshan, B., and F. Deneen. *Internet (and more) for kids.* Alameda, Calif.: Sybex, 1994.

*Learning and Leading with Technology* (formerly *The Computing Teacher*). International Society for Technology in Education. 1787 Agate Street, Eugene, OR 97403-1923. Published eight times a year. For additional information: **ISTE@oregon.uoregon.edu**

Levine, S. L. *Promoting adult growth in schools: The promise of professional development.* Boston: Allyn & Bacon, 1989.

Mager, R. F. *Making instruction work.* Belmont, Calif.: David S. Lake, 1988.

――. *Measuring instructional results.* Belmont, Calif.: David S. Lake, 1973.

――. *Preparing instructional objectives.* Palo Alto, Calif.: Fearon, 1962.

"Make the Web work in your curriculum: How three innovative schools use the Web to enhance education." *Classroom Connect* 2, no. 7 (1996), 1– .

Maxwell, C., and C. J. Grycz. *The New Riders' official Internet yellow pages.* Indianapolis, Ind.: New Riders Publishing, 1994.

McCabe, P. P. 1984. "Stretch your budgets: Have schools and public libraries cooperate." *Journal of Reading* 27(7): 632–35.

Miller, J., B. Cassie, and S. Drake. *Holistic learning: A teacher's guide to integrated studies.* Toronto: OISE Press, 1990.

Miller, S. E. *Civilizing cyberspace: Policy, power, and the information superhighway.* New York: ACM Press/Reading, Mass.: Addison-Wesley, 1996.

Morville, P., L. B. Rosenfeld, and J. Janes. *The Internet searcher's handbook.* New York: Neal-Schuman, 1995.

Moursund, D., and D. Ricketts. *Long-range planning for computers in schools.* Eugene, Oreg.: Information Age Education, 1987.

*MultiMedia Schools.* Online Inc. 462 Danbury Road, Wilton, CT 06897-2126. Published five times a year. For additional information: **Gopher://online.lib.uic.edu**

*Online Educator.* Online Publications, Inc. P.O. Box 251141, West Bloomfield, MI 48325. Published monthly during the school year. Also available in an e-mail version. To subscribe, send your name, address, and preference for the e-mail or printed version to: **ednetnews@aol.com**
For additional information. **http://ole.net/ole/**

Paterson, J. L. *Leadership for tomorrow's schools.* Alexandria, Va.: Association for Supervision and Curriculum Development, 1993.

*Pathways to School Improvement* [on-line].
Available WWW: **http://www.ncrel.org/**
Path: **ncrel/sdrs/**
File: **pathwayg.htm**

Perrone, V., ed. *Expanding student assessment.* Alexandria, Va.: Association for Supervision and Curriculum Development, 1991.

Pfaffenberger, B. *World Wide Web Bible.* New York: MIS Press, 1995.

Piaget, J. *The child's conception of the world.* London: Routledge & Kegan Paul, 1929.

――. *The theory of stages in cognitive development.* New York: McGraw-Hill, 1975.

Pike, M. A., P. Kent, K. Husain, D. Kinnaman, and D. C. Menges. *Using MOSAIC.* Indianapolis, Ind.: Que Corporation, 1994.

Plunkett, L. C., and A. G. Hale. *The proactive manager.* New York: John Wiley & Sons, 1982.

Popham, W. J. *Educational evaluation.* Englewood Cliffs, N.J.: Prentice-Hall, 1975.

Posner, G., and A. Rudnitsky. *Course design.* New York: Longman, 1986.

Protheroe, N., and E. Wilson. *The Internet handbook for school users.* Arlington, Va.: Educational Research Service, 1994.

――. *The Internet manual for classroom use.* Arlington, Va.: Educational Research Service, 1994.

Rheingold, H. *The virtual community: Homesteading on the electronic frontier.* Reading, Mass.: Addison-Wesley, 1993.

Sagor, R. *How to conduct collaborative research.* Alexandria, Va.: Association for
    Supervision and Curriculum Development, 1992.

———. "Overcoming the one-solution syndrome." *Educational Leadership* 52, no. 7 (1995):
    24–27.

Saphier, J., and M. King. "Good seeds grow in strong cultures." *Educational Leadership* 42,
    no. 6 (1985): 67–74.

Sarason, S. B. *The culture of the school and the problem of change.* 2d ed. Boston: Allyn &
    Bacon, 1982.

Schlechty, P. C. *Schools for the 21st century: Leadership imperatives for educational
    reform.* San Francisco: Jossey-Bass, 1990.

Schneider, K. G. *The Internet access cookbook: A librarian's commonsense guide to
    low-cost connections.* New York: Neal-Schuman, 1995.

Senge, P. M. *The fifth discipline: The art and practice of the learning organization.* New
    York: Doubleday/Currency, 1990.

Sheingold, K., and M. Tucker, eds. *Restructuring for learning with technology.* New York:
    Center for Technology in Education/Rochester, N.Y.: National Center on Education and
    the Economy, 1990.

Simpson, C. M. *Internet for library media specialists.* Worthington, Ohio: Linworth, 1995.

Smith, M. F. *Evaluability assessment: A practical approach.* Boston: Kluwer, 1989.

Swick, K. J. 1992. *Teacher-parent partnerships.* ERIC Digest. EDRS No. 351 149.

*Syllabus.* Syllabus Press. 1307 South Mary Avenue, Suite 211, Sunnyvale, CA 94087.
    Published ten times a year. For additional information: **info@syllabus.com** or
    **http://www.syllabus.com/**

Taba, H. *Curriculum development: Theory and practice.* New York: Harcourt, Brace & World,
    1962.

*Technology Connection.* Linworth Publishing, Inc. 40 East Wilson Bridge Road, Suite L,
    Worthington, OH 43085-2372. Published ten times during the school year. e-mail:
    **newslin.@aol.com**
    For additional information: **http://www.infomall.org/Showcase/Linworth/**

Tyler, R. W. *Basic principles of curriculum instruction.* Chicago: University of Chicago Press,
    1950.

Weir, S. 1992. *Electronic communities of learners: Fact or fiction.* Cambridge, Mass.:
    Technology Education Research Centers.

Willis, S. "Putting research to use: By heeding research findings, practitioners can make
    informed judgments." *ASCD Update* 36, no. 6 (1994): 6.

———. "Teachers as researchers: Educators use 'action research' to improve practices."
    *ASCD Update* 37, no. 3 (1995): 1– .

HotWired, 83
HTML. *See* Hypertext Markup Language
Hypermedia, 96
Hypertext Markup Language (HTML), 96,
97–98, 109–10
Hytelnet, 96

ICONnect, 69, 78
ILS. *See* Integrated learning system
Infoseek, 100, 101, 103, 107
Integrated learning system (ILS), 46, 49
Intellectual freedom, 78
Internet, xvii–xviii, 7, 12–13. *See also*
Acceptable use policies, World Wide
Web
access to, 3, 63, 78–79, 80, 84
connection to, 12, 49, 55, 98, 100,
113
educational use of, xv–xvi, 60, 64
educational value of, 55–56
functions, 9–10
integration into curriculum, 77, 104
organization of, 7
timelines, 12, 13
tools, 95–96, 113
Internet Explorer, 9, 96
Internet Relay Chat (IRC), 10
*Internet Resource Directory for Educators
(IRD)*, 68
Internet resources
citing, 141–47
demonstrating, xix
for education, 130, 118
Internet service providers (ISPs), 12, 14,
16, 17
ISDN lines, 17, 18

Java, 10

Kane, Thomas, 131
Kermit, 118–19
Keyword searches, 10
Keywords, 100, 101, 117, 129
Kostner, Martjin, 103

LANs, 8, 14, 15
Leadership, 2, 4–7, 19, 57, 60–61, 74
Librarians. *See* Media librarians
Libraries, 3, 4, 6–7. *See also* Library
media programs
public, 43, 52
Library automation, 51–52
*Library Bill of Rights*, 79
Library catalogs, 124–25
Library media programs, 5
community links, 42, 51–52
functions, 6, 7
mission statement, 29
public library links, 43, 51
public relations for, 42–43
Library of Congress, 3, 70
Licenses, 45, 50
Listservs, 10, 121–23, 130
citation style, 144
education-related resources, 108
intellectual freedom, 78
queries to, 35
staff development, 67
Literature sites, 3
Local area networks (LANs), 8, 14, 15
Lycos, 100, 101, 103
Lynx, 9, 53, 98, 113

Magid, Lawrence, 88
Mailing lists, 9
Mailservs. *See* Listservs
Maintenance (networks), 15
Massachusetts Software Council, 25, 35
Math education sites, 5
McKenzie, Jamie, 28, 32, 69, 85
Media librarians
as change agents, xv, xvii
as community liaison, 45
ethical information use, 91–92
information access expertise, 4, 6,
44, 45
as leaders in technology use, 4–7,
19, 57, 60–61, 74
licensing tasks, 50

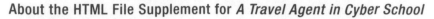

## About the HTML File Supplement for *A Travel Agent in Cyber School*

The disks on the inside back cover contain HTML files that provide links to the resources discussed in this book. As you read *A Travel Agent in Cyber School*, you can use these HTML files to connect directly to the resources referenced in the text.

### Instructions for Using the Disks

1. Insert the disk in the floppy disk drive of your computer.

2. Connect to the Internet in your usual way.

3. Open your World Wide Web browser.

4. In your Web browser, open the file

**tagent.htm**

For example, in Netscape, pull down the File menu and choose the command Open File. In the Open File dialog box, select the floppy disk drive in which you have inserted the disk, then select the file **tagent.htm**. Then click on the "Open" or "OK" button.

5. The home page will appear on your screen. Click on any chapter listed to get a list of Internet resources referenced in that chapter.

6. A list of resources will appear on your screen. Click on any resource to access it.

### Additional Tips

It's a good idea to make a backup copy of the floppy disk before using it for the first time.

You may wish to copy the contents of the floppy disk to a folder/directory on your hard drive. To use the files after copying them to the hard drive, simply open your Web browser, select the folder/directory you created to hold the files, then select tagent.htm from the list of files in that folder/directory.

If you find that a resource has moved since the HTML file supplement was created, you may wish to enter the new address as a bookmark so you can return directly to the new address at another time. Consult your browser's Help function for more information about creating bookmarks.

### Copying Restriction

The disks included with this book may be copied one time for back-up purposes only.